CW01497461

■ Copyright & Disclaimer

Football Inc.: How Billionaires Bought the World's Game
© 2025 ND Publishing
All rights reserved.

Disclaimer

This book is a work of nonfiction. Every effort has been made to ensure the accuracy of information presented. Facts, names, figures, and public events are drawn from publicly available, verified sources. Any interpretations, analyses, or opinions expressed are those of the author and are intended for informational and educational purposes only.

The author and publisher make no representations or warranties regarding the completeness, reliability, or accuracy of this information and disclaim any liability for actions taken based on it.

All trademarks, service marks, product names, and company names mentioned are the property of their respective owners and are used for identification purposes only. Their inclusion does not imply any affiliation, endorsement, or sponsorship.

ISBN: 9798269349404

Introduction – The Beautiful Game Turns Corporate

From Muddy Pitches to Million-Dollar Deals

It started with a ball, a patch of grass, and a crowd that lived for Saturday afternoons. For most of the twentieth century, football belonged to the people — a game for factory workers, students, and dreamers. The chants, the scarves, the community spirit: that was what defined the sport. But somewhere between the terraces and the television cameras, between the heart and the hedge funds, something shifted.

Football didn't just grow; it exploded. It became a global commodity — a product as much as a passion. The same sport once fueled by local pride and homegrown talent now moves billions in broadcast revenue, sponsorships, and global marketing. Clubs that used to be neighborhood institutions now double as international corporations, complete with CEOs, brand managers, and digital marketing departments.

The transformation didn't happen overnight. It was the result of decades of financial evolution — and, depending on who you ask, financial corruption. It began with television rights, accelerated with sponsorship deals, and reached new heights when billionaires and oil-rich states joined the game. Today, owning a football club isn't just about sport. It's about power, prestige, and sometimes, politics.

The Day the Game Changed

On February 20th, 1992, in a London hotel, the chairmen of England's biggest clubs met to finalize a breakaway league — one that would allow them to sell their own broadcast rights. It was the birth of the **Premier League**, a name that would soon symbolize both sporting excellence and corporate dominance.

That summer, Rupert Murdoch's Sky Sports paid £304 million for the right to broadcast matches for five years. To the public, it looked like an ambitious TV deal. To insiders, it was the start of a revolution. Suddenly, football wasn't just a pastime; it was prime-time entertainment. And for the first time, the game's financial ceiling disappeared.

Sky's investment triggered an arms race. More cameras, better stadiums, international players — all designed to attract a global audience. Stadiums filled with tourists from Asia and America, broadcasting deals stretched across continents, and clubs realized they could sell not just tickets but *stories*. Football became entertainment, and fans became customers.

Globalization: The New Kickoff

By the early 2000s, football had gone global. The Premier League became a household name in Singapore, New York, and Nairobi. Jerseys were no longer just symbols of loyalty — they were fashion statements. A child in Bangkok could support Manchester United as passionately as someone from Salford.

This global reach created a gold rush. Investors saw that football had the two things every business dreams of: emotion and loyalty. No other industry could make millions of people cry over a single result, then do it again next week. Clubs became brands, players became influencers, and stadiums became platforms for political and commercial power.

That's when the billionaires arrived.

When Money Met the Beautiful Game

In 2003, Russian oligarch **Roman Abramovich** bought Chelsea FC for around £140 million. He cleared the club's debts and spent another £100 million on players in his first transfer window. It was football's "Big Bang" moment — the signal that the sport had entered a new era of private wealth.

Abramovich didn't just buy a club; he bought credibility, influence, and global recognition. His Chelsea takeover changed everything. Within five years, English football was crawling with billionaires: the Glazer family in Manchester, Sheikh Mansour in Abu Dhabi, Stan Kroenke in London,

John Henry in Liverpool. Each had their own reasons — but all saw football as the perfect investment vehicle.

The results were staggering. Club valuations soared, sponsorship deals reached into the hundreds of millions, and transfer fees defied logic. The game that once struggled to pay wages was now generating billions in global revenue. But behind the glamour came something more unsettling: the quiet replacement of community ownership with corporate control.

Fans became spectators not just of matches but of financial takeovers, court cases, and brand announcements. The game's vocabulary changed — "net spend," "market value," "revenue streams" — words that belonged in boardrooms, not locker rooms.

From Oligarchs to Oil States

Then came a new kind of owner — not just rich individuals, but entire nations. In 2008, **Sheikh Mansour bin Zayed Al Nahyan** of Abu Dhabi bought Manchester City. In 2011, **Qatar Sports Investments** took over Paris Saint-Germain. In 2021, **Saudi Arabia's Public Investment Fund** acquired Newcastle United.

This wasn't just investment; it was geopolitics. Football became an instrument of **soft power**, a way for states to shape global perception. Stadiums turned into billboards for national identity. For Abu Dhabi, Qatar, and Saudi Arabia, the sport offered something priceless: credibility and connection with billions of fans around the world.

Critics call it **sportswashing** — using sport to mask human rights issues and political controversies. Supporters call it progress — modern infrastructure, new jobs, and international prestige. Both are true. Football has become a stage where business, image, and politics intersect like never before.

The Changing Face of Ownership

By the 2020s, the modern football map looked more like a corporate chart than a league table. American funds owned multiple European clubs, City Football Group managed a network of teams across five continents, and brands from Qatar to Japan sponsored shirts, stadiums, and training kits.

The sport's ecosystem had evolved into a multi-trillion-dollar industry. Broadcast rights, digital streaming, and online merchandise expanded football's reach beyond imagination. The average Premier League club is now worth over £1 billion, while top players command salaries exceeding £20 million per year.

But this success came with a paradox. The more global football became, the further it drifted from its roots. Local fans were priced out of matches. Clubs with 100 years of tradition now answered to foreign boards. And while the money brought trophies, it also deepened inequality between the elite and everyone else.

The romantic notion of "any club can win" became a myth. Wealth dictated results. The league table mirrored the balance sheet.

The Fans Caught in the Middle

Despite all the upheaval, fans have never been more invested — literally and emotionally. They fill stadiums, buy subscriptions, and argue online in every language imaginable. Football remains an obsession that transcends politics and borders.

But the soul of the game feels contested. Supporters have protested takeovers, boycotted matches, and launched fan-owned movements in resistance to the corporate tide. From Manchester United's "Green and Gold" campaign to Newcastle supporters divided over Saudi ownership, every major club has faced the same question: *Who really owns football?*

The answer is complicated. The people who love it don't own it. The people who can afford it often don't love it.

Why This Book Matters

Football Inc. is about understanding this new world — the billionaires, the empires, and the empires behind the billionaires. It's about tracing the money, unpacking the power, and explaining why this matters to anyone who still cares about the game itself.

Each chapter will explore a piece of the puzzle: how global ownership models emerged, how clubs turned into brands, how fans fought back, and how football became the most visible symbol of globalization itself. We'll look at the business side, the human stories, and the political games being played behind the scenes.

This isn't a nostalgic lament for a lost era. It's an honest examination of how the world's most beloved sport became the world's most lucrative business — and what that means for its future.

The Stakes

The central tension in modern football is simple: passion versus profit. The game thrives because of its unpredictability, but its economics reward predictability. Billionaires want returns; fans want miracles. And as money tightens its grip, those miracles are becoming rarer.

Yet, amid the billion-dollar deals and boardroom drama, something remarkable endures. Every weekend, millions still gather in pubs, living rooms, and stadiums. They still shout, hope, and believe. For ninety minutes, no matter who owns the club or how much they paid, football still belongs to them.

A New Era, the Same Game

We stand at a crossroads. The global football economy has never been stronger — but its moral and cultural foundation has never been weaker. The sport's future depends on whether balance can be restored between business and belief, between profit and passion.

In the pages that follow, we'll explore how football got here, who's really in charge, and whether the beautiful game can remain beautiful in the age of billionaires.

Because for all the money in the world, football's true value still comes from something that can't be bought: emotion.

And as long as fans keep singing, maybe — just maybe — the game isn't lost yet.

Chapter 1 – The Rise of Football as Big Business

A New Beginning in 1992

In 1992, the English football landscape changed forever. After years of declining stadium attendances, crumbling infrastructure, and violent hooliganism, the country's top clubs decided to break away from the Football League and form their own elite competition — the **Premier League**.

At the time, it was sold to fans as a modernization effort. In reality, it was the dawn of football as a business empire. The breakaway was driven by a single, powerful idea: clubs could make far more money by selling broadcast rights directly, instead of sharing them with the lower divisions.

That same year, **Sky Television**, owned by media tycoon Rupert Murdoch, made an audacious move. The company paid **£304 million** for a five-year deal to broadcast Premier League matches — a record-breaking figure that seemed almost absurd at the time. Before that, the BBC and ITV had offered around £44 million.

The Sky deal changed everything. Football went from a weekend hobby to a 24-hour product. It wasn't just a sport anymore; it was television content, prime-time drama, and global marketing rolled into one.

Within a few seasons, the transformation was visible. Stadiums became safer, broadcast coverage became cinematic, and footballers became celebrities. The league's slick presentation drew millions of new fans, not just in England but across Asia, Africa, and North America. Football's global era had begun.

The Birth of a Money Machine

The success of the Premier League didn't just reshape English football — it reshaped global sports economics. Sky's gamble paid off spectacularly. Subscriber numbers soared, advertisers lined up, and television became football's main source of income.

By 1997, Sky renewed its deal for **£670 million**, and by 2001, it was paying **£1.2 billion**. What started as a bold investment had become a gold rush. The other leagues in Europe took notice. Spain's La Liga, Italy's Serie A, and Germany's Bundesliga began selling their own rights in record sums, inspired by the English model.

Television wasn't just a way to show matches; it became the sport's economic engine. Every broadcast meant exposure. Every exposure meant sponsorship. Soon, global brands — from beer companies to airlines — were fighting for a place on club shirts and billboards.

Football had discovered its ultimate product: emotion. Every fan's joy, heartbreak, and tribal loyalty could be monetized.

Manchester United: The First Global Brand

No club understood this better than **Manchester United**. Under manager **Sir Alex Ferguson** and chief executive **Peter Kenyon**, United turned success on the pitch into dominance off it. The club became the first football brand to truly go global.

By 1999, the year United won the historic treble (Premier League, FA Cup, and Champions League), the club had sponsorships with Nike, Vodafone, and Sharp. Its merchandise sold in over 60 countries. The team's tours across Asia and the United States filled stadiums with fans who had never set foot in Manchester.

United's model became a template for others. The club listed on the London Stock Exchange, released branded credit cards, and pioneered direct marketing to fans. For the first time, a football club was being run like a multinational corporation.

Football Becomes a Global Export

The globalization of football followed the same pattern as entertainment industries like film and music. What Hollywood was to movies, the Premier League became to sport. Matches were broadcast live to hundreds of countries. Clubs launched official websites in multiple languages.

By the early 2000s, the Premier League had overtaken the Italian Serie A and Spanish La Liga as the world's most lucrative league. Its international TV rights deals were worth billions. The league's popularity in Asia, particularly in **China, Japan, and Malaysia**, created new fanbases that local clubs could only dream of.

Soon, global ownership began to follow global audiences. Wealthy investors realized that a football club was not just a sports team — it was a marketing platform with access to hundreds of millions of consumers.

The Economics of the Modern Game

Football's new economy was built on three pillars: **broadcast revenue, sponsorship, and matchday income**.

- **Broadcast rights** became the backbone. In 1992, the average Premier League club earned less than £1 million a year from TV money. By 2020, that figure exceeded £100 million for most top-tier clubs.

- **Sponsorships** multiplied. Shirt sponsors, sleeve sponsors, official training kit partners — every inch of fabric and advertising space could be sold.

- **Matchday income** evolved. Clubs began offering luxury boxes, executive lounges, and "corporate hospitality experiences" instead of just season tickets.

Together, these revenue streams created an ecosystem where football's biggest clubs operated like Fortune 500 companies. Financial analysts tracked their balance sheets, fans debated annual reports, and Forbes published yearly rankings of "The World's Most Valuable Football Teams."

The Divide Grows

But with great wealth came great inequality. The top clubs — Manchester United, Arsenal, Liverpool, Chelsea — grew exponentially richer, while smaller sides struggled to keep up.

Before the Premier League era, an underdog could realistically challenge for the title. Nottingham Forest and Derby County did it in the 1970s. Leeds United and Blackburn Rovers managed it in the 1990s. But by the 2000s, the concentration of money made such fairytales nearly impossible.

Television money wasn't distributed equally, and success created self-reinforcing cycles of wealth. The clubs that qualified for the Champions League reaped even more TV income, more sponsorships, and more fans — allowing them to buy better players and stay at the top.

Football had entered an **age of financial stratification**. The sport's new elite were not just good teams — they were global corporations with marketing departments, analytics teams, and billion-dollar valuations.

When Winning Meets Business

This financial boom created a strange paradox. The more money poured into the game, the more predictable it became. Clubs once defined by risk-taking now ran like risk-averse corporations. Every decision was weighed not just in footballing terms but in financial impact.

Signing a player wasn't just about improving the squad — it was about growing the brand. A superstar from Asia or the U.S. could increase merchandise sales, social media followers, and international partnerships. Clubs began signing sponsorships based on players' nationalities rather than their performance potential.

The sport's emotional authenticity began to erode. Fans who had grown up standing in freezing stadiums now watched their teams play summer friendlies in Los Angeles and Tokyo. It was football, but it wasn't *their* football anymore.

UEFA's Role: The Champions League Effect

Meanwhile, in Europe, UEFA's **Champions League** became another financial superpower. Its prize money and broadcasting deals dwarfed domestic competitions. The top clubs realized that qualification was worth tens of millions annually — failure meant economic disaster.

This turned the Champions League into both a financial lifeline and a weapon. The rich stayed rich because they could afford to qualify; the rest were left behind.

By 2019, the financial gap between Europe's elite and the rest had become astronomical. Clubs like Real Madrid, Barcelona, Bayern Munich, and the Premier League's top six were operating on budgets that smaller teams couldn't dream of matching. The pyramid was tipping dangerously toward monopoly.

The Legacy of the Premier League Model

Thirty years on, the Premier League remains the world's richest league — a global juggernaut generating more than £6 billion annually. Its model of centralized broadcasting, aggressive global marketing, and private investment has been copied by leagues from the United States to the Middle East.

But the cost of success has been cultural. Many traditional fans feel alienated by the commercialization of their sport. The chants, the traditions, and even the kickoff times have changed — all to suit broadcasters and sponsors.

The Premier League sold its soul for global relevance, critics say. Yet the numbers don't lie: attendances are higher, global reach is wider, and revenues are stronger than ever. For every fan who mourns the past, there are millions worldwide who fell in love with the sport because of its new accessibility.

From Local Clubs to Global Assets

The rise of football as big business set the stage for what came next: the billionaire era. Once clubs were profitable, they became valuable. Once they became valuable, they became targets.

Private investors, oligarchs, and later, entire nation-states saw football clubs as tools of influence — trophies of a new kind. They could buy history, legitimacy, and a slice of cultural power.

The Premier League's financial model made that possible. Its global popularity turned even mid-table clubs into billion-pound assets. For investors seeking both prestige and profit, there was no better buy.

The Turning Point

By the early 2000s, the football world had been transformed. Players were multimillionaires. Agents were power brokers. Clubs had marketing teams larger than their scouting departments. The game had become a global media product.

And yet, for all the money and modernization, something essential had changed. Football was no longer just a sport played by teams — it was a market traded by empires.

That's where our story truly begins. Because the next chapter isn't about the rise of the Premier League — it's about who bought it.

The billionaires were coming. And they wouldn't just change football's finances — they would change its very identity.

Chapter 2 – Enter the Billionaires

The Day Football Went Platinum

It was a gray July morning in 2003 when a modest press release from west London changed football forever. *"Chelsea Football Club is pleased to confirm that it has agreed terms with Roman Abramovich for the sale of the club."*

Most fans barely knew who he was. Within 24 hours, they found out. Abramovich — a Russian oligarch whose fortune came from oil and aluminum — had just spent around **£140 million** to buy Chelsea. A few weeks later, he splashed another **£100 million** on new players, shattering transfer records and rewriting football's power structure overnight.

Chelsea went from a respected London club to one of the world's richest sporting institutions almost instantly. Fans couldn't believe it. Rival supporters couldn't ignore it. The era of the football billionaire had begun.

The Oligarch Blueprint

Abramovich's Chelsea wasn't just about trophies — it was about transformation. His takeover proved that money could rewrite football history in real time. In his first two years, Chelsea won back-to-back Premier League titles, ending decades of underachievement.

The formula was simple but effective: heavy investment, elite management, and a long-term vision. But what made Abramovich's move revolutionary was the *why*. He wasn't buying a business for profit — he was buying global influence.

In post-Soviet Russia, oligarchs often sought legitimacy and visibility abroad. A Premier League club was the perfect vehicle. It offered global reach, public image, and access to the British establishment. It wasn't just football — it was soft power before the term became fashionable.

Abramovich's success inspired others. If one man could transform a club with cash, imagine what could happen if an entire class of billionaires entered the game. And they did — from Wall Street to the Middle East.

The Glazers and the American Model

Two years later, in 2005, the **Glazer family**, owners of the NFL's Tampa Bay Buccaneers, launched a **leveraged buyout** of Manchester United. The concept shocked traditionalists. The Glazers didn't buy the club with cash — they borrowed against it, saddling United with nearly **£600 million** in debt.

Fans revolted. Thousands protested outside Old Trafford, waving banners that read *"Love United, Hate Glazer."* Some formed a breakaway club, **FC United of Manchester**, as a grassroots protest.

But the Glazers weren't sentimental. They saw football as a mature entertainment industry — much like American sports. The goal wasn't just to win trophies; it was to maximize global revenue. United's brand was strong enough to generate profits despite the debt.

Under their model, commercial partnerships exploded. From regional noodle sponsors in Asia to car deals in the U.S., Manchester United became the world's most marketable sports brand. By 2013, the club's annual revenue surpassed **£430 million**, and its valuation hit **$3 billion** — more than many NFL franchises.

Fans hated the corporate feel. Investors loved it. United had become the perfect hybrid: a football club operating like a multinational corporation.

The Americans Take Over

The Glazers weren't alone. American investors were drawn to football for the same reason they were drawn to tech startups — rapid growth and global potential.

In 2007, **Stan Kroenke**, owner of the Denver Nuggets and Colorado Rapids, began buying shares in Arsenal. By 2011, he became majority owner. His philosophy was clear: sustainability over sentimentality. Arsenal would live within its means, even if that meant fewer trophies.

Supporters mocked his hands-off approach, calling him "Silent Stan." But Kroenke's business logic was unshakable. The value of Arsenal's brand doubled within a decade.

Meanwhile, in 2010, **John Henry** and the **Fenway Sports Group (FSG)** acquired Liverpool. Their background in baseball's Boston Red Sox taught them the power of analytics and data-driven recruitment. They hired experts to optimize transfers, embraced technology, and focused on building long-term stability.

Their model paid off spectacularly. By 2019, Liverpool won both the Champions League and Premier League. But perhaps more importantly for FSG, the club's value tripled. Henry once told *The Boston Globe*, "We don't buy trophies — we build systems."

The message was clear: football ownership wasn't about passion anymore. It was about *strategy*.

Billionaires, Politics, and Prestige

Every billionaire enters football for a reason — and it's rarely just the love of the game.

For Abramovich, it was international legitimacy. For the Glazers, diversification. For Kroenke, a low-risk asset with high upside. For Abu Dhabi's Sheikh Mansour, it was national branding (a story we'll explore in Chapter 3).

Football provided what no other investment could: instant cultural relevance. A tech mogul can build apps that reach millions, but owning a club makes headlines every weekend. The global exposure is unmatched

In business terms, football clubs offer a unique combination of scarcity and visibility. There are only so many elite clubs in the world, and they attract billions of viewers annually. That makes them ideal vehicles for billionaires seeking both status and influence.

Changing the Culture of Clubs

The influx of billionaire ownership didn't just change the economics — it changed the culture.

Boardrooms replaced community halls. Supporters who once felt connected to their clubs now watched decisions made in boardrooms thousands of miles away. Ticket prices rose as clubs chased premium audiences. Local fans became background noise in a global business.

Yet, paradoxically, these owners often saved clubs from financial ruin. Before Abramovich, Chelsea faced bankruptcy. Before FSG, Liverpool was drowning in debt under previous owners Hicks and Gillett. Billionaires didn't just buy teams — they stabilized them, rebranded them, and made them global again.

The trade-off was clear: **security for sovereignty**. Clubs that once belonged to their towns now belonged to tycoons.

The Numbers Behind the Revolution

Between 2003 and 2023, foreign ownership in the Premier League exploded. In 2000, only three of the 20 clubs had non-British owners. Today, **16 out of 20** are foreign-owned. Collectively, Premier League clubs are worth more than **£30 billion**.

This shift wasn't limited to England. In Italy, American investors now control clubs like AC Milan, Roma, and Fiorentina. In France, Qatar owns Paris Saint-Germain. In Spain, investment funds hover around clubs like vultures, waiting for openings.

Football has become part of the **global capital network**, where hedge funds, oil empires, and private investors all play the same game — but with different end goals.

Winners and Losers

For some fans, billionaire ownership brought dreams to life. Chelsea's success under Abramovich created lifelong memories. Manchester City's rise under Sheikh Mansour turned despair into dominance. Liverpool's revival under FSG reconnected a city to its glory days.

But for others, the price was too high. The game became less competitive. The romance of underdog victories faded. Clubs like Burnley or Brentford could never compete financially, no matter how smartly they were run.

Money didn't just influence outcomes — it dictated them.

The financial gap became structural. Billionaires had built moats around their clubs, protected by commercial power and global fanbases. Smaller teams were locked out of the elite circle, destined to fight for survival instead of titles.

The Football Billionaires Club

By the 2010s, football's richest owners formed an exclusive club of their own. The top tier included oligarchs, tycoons, and sheikhs whose combined wealth exceeded **$500 billion**.

They didn't just control clubs — they controlled narratives. They sat on boards, influenced regulations, and reshaped the sport's governance to suit their interests.

It wasn't unusual anymore for a billionaire's private jet to touch down on transfer deadline day, sign a player worth £100 million, and take off again within hours. What was once unimaginable had become normal.

Football wasn't being played just on the pitch — it was being negotiated in boardrooms, embassies, and investment meetings.

A Changing Definition of Success

In this new era, success took on new meanings. Trophies were still important, but so were *valuations*. Clubs bragged as much about their brand rankings and follower counts as their goals scored.

A Champions League victory could raise a club's market value by hundreds of millions. A star signing wasn't just a football decision — it was a marketing move. When Manchester United signed Cristiano Ronaldo in 2021, the club gained over 10 million new social media followers within a week and saw a surge in merchandise sales.

The billionaire era blurred the lines between sport, media, and finance. Clubs were no longer measured solely in goals, but in growth.

Fan Power Diminished

The arrival of billionaire owners also revealed how little power traditional fans actually held. Protests became common — from Manchester United's pitch invasions to Arsenal supporters marching outside the Emirates. But in the face of global capital, their influence was minimal.

The average supporter couldn't compete with an oligarch's wealth or a sovereign fund's resources. Fan voices were symbolic, not strategic.

Football's democratic spirit — the idea that it belonged to the people — was now competing with the cold reality of corporate control.

The Era of the Global Elite

By the end of the 2010s, billionaire ownership wasn't just normal — it was expected. The Premier League's global dominance, combined with its open ownership laws, made it irresistible to investors.

For some, it was business. For others, it was image. For all, it was power.

The game that once relied on community spirit had become a theater for global ambition. Clubs were no longer defined by their cities but by the wealth and politics of their owners.

The sport had entered a new phase — one that blurred the line between private investment and state control.

And that's where the next chapter begins.

Because if billionaires could reshape football's business, imagine what would happen when nations — armed with oil money, diplomacy, and strategy — decided to buy the game itself.

Chapter 3 – Oil Money and Power Plays

A Sky-Blue Revolution

On September 1, 2008, football woke up to a new world. Overnight, **Manchester City** had gone from a mid-table Premier League side to the richest club on the planet. The reason? A deal quietly finalized in Abu Dhabi. Sheikh Mansour bin Zayed Al Nahyan—member of the Emirati royal family and deputy prime minister of the United Arab Emirates—had bought the club through the newly formed **Abu Dhabi United Group**.

Hours later, City announced the signing of Brazilian star **Robinho** from Real Madrid for a British-record £32.5 million. Cameras swarmed the Etihad; reporters called it "the day football changed." The symbolism was perfect: a new dawn colored in oil money blue.

For decades, City had lived in Manchester United's shadow. Now, they had something United didn't—near-unlimited funding backed by a state with global ambitions. The takeover wasn't just about trophies; it was about image, diplomacy, and identity. Abu Dhabi wanted to project itself as modern, progressive, and open for business. Football was the fastest way to do it.

Football as Soft Power

Political scientists call it **soft power**—the ability to influence others through attraction rather than coercion. The United States does it with Hollywood. Japan does it with technology and pop culture. The Gulf states chose football.

The UAE, Qatar, and later Saudi Arabia understood that Western audiences who might ignore their trade expos or policy reforms would eagerly watch a 90-minute match. If those audiences associated their nations with beautiful football rather than oil rigs or politics, that was a win.

Sheikh Mansour's purchase came during the global financial crisis, when Western economies were wobbling. To many in Abu Dhabi, the move symbolized confidence—a demonstration that Gulf capital could stabilize what the West was losing control of.

Manchester City quickly became a global marketing vehicle. Etihad Airways, owned by the Abu Dhabi government, signed a record shirt and stadium sponsorship reportedly worth over £400 million. The **City Football Group (CFG)** soon followed, purchasing or founding clubs in New York, Melbourne, Girona, Mumbai, and Montevideo. A football network had replaced the old colonial trade routes.

The State Behind the Club

Critics asked the obvious question: *was this still sport?* When a team is funded by a sovereign wealth fund, can it truly compete on equal terms?

UEFA tried to impose **Financial Fair Play (FFP)** rules in 2011 to limit reckless spending, but enforcement proved weak. State-backed teams had legal armies and sponsorship structures designed to stay technically compliant while still injecting massive resources. The playing field tilted sharply.

Manchester City built the **Etihad Campus**, a £200 million training complex with hydrotherapy pools, cryo-chambers, and data centers. They hired top executives from Barcelona and Real Madrid. By 2023, City had won multiple Premier League titles and the Champions League. The sporting achievement was real—but inseparable from the billions of petro-dollars behind it.

For Abu Dhabi, the investment delivered returns far beyond trophies. The city's name became synonymous with excellence rather than excess. Tourism increased. Western universities and companies opened partnerships in the emirate. The football club had done its job: rewrite perception.

Enter Qatar: The Paris Project

If Abu Dhabi's move was strategic, Qatar's was spectacular. In 2011, **Qatar Sports Investments (QSI)**—a subsidiary of the country's sovereign wealth fund—bought **Paris Saint-Germain**. Overnight, PSG went from a fashionable but inconsistent French club to a global super-brand.

The timing was no accident. Qatar had just won the bid to host the **2022 FIFA World Cup**, the first ever held in the Middle East. Owning a European powerhouse would keep the country in the headlines for the next decade and showcase its financial might.

PSG's spending spree made headlines year after year:

- **Zlatan Ibrahimović** in 2012 for £20 million.

- **David Beckham**'s short-term arrival in 2013, pure publicity genius.

- Then the record-shattering **Neymar** transfer in 2017 for €222 million, followed by **Kylian Mbappé** for €180 million.

These moves weren't just football decisions—they were global marketing campaigns. PSG's social-media following exploded from 2 million to over 100 million within a decade. The club became a walking advertisement for "Brand Qatar."

Yet the controversy never faded. Human-rights organizations accused Qatar of using football to distract from labor abuses and lack of democratic reform. The term **sportswashing** entered mainstream vocabulary, describing how regimes polish their image through sport.

The Saudi Play

By the early 2020s, **Saudi Arabia**—the largest and most powerful Gulf state—decided it couldn't be left out. In 2021, its **Public Investment**

Fund (PIF), chaired by Crown Prince Mohammed bin Salman, acquired an 80 percent stake in **Newcastle United**.

For Newcastle fans, worn down by years of mediocrity under previous owner Mike Ashley, the deal felt like salvation. Within months, investment poured into the club's infrastructure, scouting, and recruitment. By 2023, Newcastle had qualified for the Champions League for the first time in two decades.

But globally, the acquisition reignited the sportswashing debate. Critics argued the purchase aimed to rebrand Saudi Arabia amid international scrutiny over human-rights issues. The government called it diversification—a step in its **Vision 2030** plan to reduce dependence on oil and build a modern, entertainment-driven economy.

The strategy extended far beyond Newcastle. The kingdom launched **LIV Golf**, hosted heavyweight boxing bouts in Jeddah, and poured money into Formula One. Football was simply the centerpiece of a broader soft-power portfolio.

The Global Ripple Effect

Oil money didn't just reshape the clubs that received it; it changed everyone else. Traditional European giants found themselves struggling to compete. AC Milan, Inter, and Borussia Dortmund couldn't match state budgets. Transfer fees and wages skyrocketed across the board.

By 2022, the average wage at a top Premier League club exceeded £100 000 per week. The arms race distorted the transfer market so dramatically that even mid-table teams spent more than champions had twenty years earlier.

UEFA's Financial Fair Play rules became a cat-and-mouse game. Regulators chased creative accounting, inflated sponsorships, and intra-group loans. Fans grew cynical; they joked that modern football had two leagues—the state-funded and everyone else.

But for all the criticism, these takeovers injected unprecedented professionalism into club management. Facilities improved, youth academies thrived, and infrastructure spending transformed local economies. Manchester's east side, once neglected, benefited from City's redevelopment projects. Paris's economy gained tourism and visibility. Even Newcastle saw job growth and urban investment.

The paradox of petro-football is clear: ethically complex, economically transformative.

The New Football Order

The rise of **state-backed teams** has created a quasi-geopolitical hierarchy inside football.

- **Manchester City** represents Abu Dhabi.

- **Paris Saint-Germain**, Qatar.

- **Newcastle United**, Saudi Arabia.

Their matches have become proxy rivalries for regional politics: oil versus gas, modernization versus tradition, influence versus image. When City meets PSG in the Champions League, it's effectively Abu Dhabi versus Doha, each seeking soft-power supremacy under UEFA floodlights.

Meanwhile, Western governments and football authorities face a dilemma. These investors bring money, jobs, and prestige—but also political baggage. Blocking them risks losing billions. Accepting them risks complicity. So most simply welcome the capital and look the other way.

Beyond the Gulf: The Domino Effect

Once Gulf wealth normalized the idea of state-backed ownership, others followed different models. Chinese conglomerates bought stakes in Italian and English clubs during the mid-2010s. American hedge funds expanded their European portfolios. Even smaller nations like Azerbaijan and Thailand entered through sponsorships.

Football had become part of the global **sovereign investment ecosystem**, where nations seek influence not only through trade and weapons but through sport and entertainment.

For fans, this meant the old distinctions between "foreign owner" and "local club" disappeared. Every major team was part of a wider economic web. Loyalty to a club now meant indirect association with a nation's foreign policy.

The Human Cost

Amid all the luxury and political theater, the human side of football has often been lost. Players became assets on balance sheets. Fans became global data points. Yet the emotional connection that makes football powerful persists.

When City fans sing "Blue Moon," they don't think about Abu Dhabi's energy strategy. When PSG ultras wave their banners, they aren't endorsing Qatari politics. But their passion is what gives those projects value. Without genuine fandom, the entire soft-power strategy collapses.

That's the quiet irony of state-backed football: the emotion it monetizes cannot be manufactured. It must be borrowed—from the people who still believe.

Power, Prestige, and the Price of Success

State money has delivered breathtaking football, global infrastructure, and commercial sophistication. But it has also blurred the boundaries between sport, business, and international relations.

The question is no longer whether oil money belongs in football—it's whether football can survive without it.

The Premier League, UEFA, and FIFA all depend on the wealth of petro-states for sponsorship, broadcasting, and investment. Any moral reckoning now threatens the entire system.

Modern football has become a geopolitical marketplace. Each goal scored under a state-funded banner doubles as a message to the world: *we belong on your stage.*

Football may still be the people's game, but the scoreboard of power now belongs to nations. And as we move deeper into this century, it's clear that the next battles for dominance won't be fought in boardrooms or parliaments—they'll be fought under floodlights.

Chapter 4 – The State Behind the Club

A Celebration and a Question

When the news broke on a crisp October evening in 2021 that the **Saudi Public Investment Fund (PIF)** had completed its takeover of **Newcastle United**, the streets around St. James' Park erupted. Flares lit the sky, fans waved Saudi flags, and strangers hugged in disbelief. After years under the unpopular ownership of Mike Ashley, it felt like liberation.

But as Newcastle supporters celebrated, journalists around the world asked a harder question: *what does it mean when a government effectively owns a football club?*

This wasn't a sponsorship deal or a private investor stepping in. The buyer was Saudi Arabia's sovereign wealth fund, chaired by Crown Prince Mohammed bin Salman. The state of Saudi Arabia, through one of the world's largest investment vehicles, had just become a major player in the Premier League.

The celebration outside the stadium captured football's modern paradox. For fans, ownership promised ambition and trophies. For critics, it raised uncomfortable issues about human rights, transparency, and political image-making.

What "State-Backed" Really Means

When we talk about "state-backed teams," we're not referring to governments issuing press releases about lineups. The reality is more sophisticated.

Most of these clubs are owned by **sovereign wealth funds (SWFs)**—government-controlled investment entities managing surplus capital, usually generated by natural resources like oil and gas. Their purpose is to diversify national income and invest in assets that generate soft power, international influence, and long-term returns.

Abu Dhabi's **Mubadala Investment Company**, Qatar's **Qatar Investment Authority**, and Saudi Arabia's **Public Investment Fund** all rank among the world's largest. Collectively, they control trillions of dollars. Football clubs are tiny pieces of their portfolios, but they're the most visible ones.

When a sovereign wealth fund owns a club, it isn't just a financial asset—it becomes part of national strategy. Each club functions as a global public-relations outlet, an advertising arm for its country's economic vision.

That's why Manchester City, PSG, and Newcastle aren't simply sports institutions. They're **geopolitical projects** with budgets that dwarf most private owners.

The Mechanics of Sportswashing

The word **sportswashing** often dominates discussions about state-backed football, but what does it actually mean?

In essence, it's the practice of using sport to improve a country's international reputation. By associating with popular clubs, hosting major tournaments, or sponsoring global events, governments aim to shift public perception—away from politics and toward prestige.

The idea isn't new. In 1936, Nazi Germany used the Berlin Olympics to project unity and strength. The Soviet Union did the same through its Olympic dominance during the Cold War. What's changed is scale and subtlety. Today's sportswashing happens through corporate channels, investment deals, and smiling photo ops rather than propaganda posters.

Football, the world's most-watched sport, is the perfect vehicle. A Champions League broadcast reaches hundreds of millions in every time zone. A club's success generates goodwill and distracts from difficult conversations about governance, human rights, or labor conditions.

Critics argue that by cheering for these teams, fans inadvertently participate in a PR campaign. Supporters counter that their loyalty is to the badge, not the boardroom. The truth lies somewhere in between.

Abu Dhabi and Manchester City: The Blueprint

When **Sheikh Mansour** purchased Manchester City in 2008, Abu Dhabi gained more than a football team—it gained a story. The emirate, often overshadowed by glitzier Dubai, wanted to position itself as a hub of innovation and stability.

City's transformation delivered exactly that narrative. Within a decade, the club built world-class facilities, won multiple league titles, and became synonymous with excellence. Every time commentators praised "the Manchester City project," they reinforced an image of Abu Dhabi as modern, competent, and forward-looking.

Meanwhile, **Etihad Airways**, owned by the Abu Dhabi government, became the club's shirt and stadium sponsor. The brand's name appeared in highlight reels, news reports, and social media feeds worldwide. Critics accused City of inflating sponsorship deals to comply with Financial Fair Play rules. The club maintained that all transactions were legitimate commercial agreements.

Either way, the strategy worked. Manchester City's rise was not only sporting dominance—it was geopolitical marketing at its most elegant.

Qatar and PSG: The Power of Image

If Abu Dhabi wrote the blueprint, **Qatar** perfected it. In 2011, **Qatar Sports Investments** took control of **Paris Saint-Germain (PSG)**. The country was already preparing to host the **2022 World Cup**, and the purchase was part of a broader vision: to make Qatar a global name synonymous with modern luxury and high performance.

PSG's spending spree shocked traditionalists. Neymar's €222 million transfer from Barcelona in 2017 broke records and symbolized an entirely new level of wealth in football. Kylian Mbappé's arrival soon after colidified the club as a modern superpower.

But beneath the glamour was a carefully orchestrated campaign. Qatar used PSG to associate itself with art, style, and sport—a far cry from the desert imagery and labor controversies dominating international headlines. The club's partnerships with Jordan Brand, Accor, and GOAT sneakers turned it into a global lifestyle label as much as a football team.

The message was subtle but clear: Qatar was small, yes, but sophisticated, creative, and capable of hosting the world's biggest events.

Saudi Arabia and Newcastle: The New Frontier

Saudi Arabia's 2021 purchase of **Newcastle United** represented the next stage in football's geopolitical evolution. Unlike its neighbors, the kingdom wasn't using sport solely to burnish its image—it was using it as a key pillar of **Vision 2030**, an economic diversification plan led by Crown Prince Mohammed bin Salman.

Football was both a domestic and international strategy. Domestically, it supported national pride and tourism; internationally, it signaled openness and reform.

Within months of the takeover, Newcastle's operations modernized. Infrastructure investment followed, jobs increased, and the team's performance improved dramatically. Fans who had endured years of neglect suddenly dreamed of silverware again.

Yet the moral tension remained. Some supporters proudly waved Saudi flags at games, seeing new ownership as a chance to compete with the elite. Others felt uneasy, arguing that passion for the club shouldn't come at the expense of ignoring political realities.

The result was a divided fanbase united only by hope—a snapshot of football's broader dilemma in the 21st century.

The Political Ripple Effect

Football's influence extends far beyond the pitch. When a state owns a club, every match becomes a subtle act of diplomacy.

In the case of Manchester City, Abu Dhabi's presence in the Premier League strengthened its ties with the UK government, fostering business deals and cultural partnerships. Qatar used PSG's popularity to build political goodwill in France and Europe. Saudi Arabia leveraged Newcastle to soften its international image and attract tourism investment.

These clubs act as informal ambassadors, building relationships that transcend embassies. Hosting a friendly match, signing a global star, or partnering with Western charities all serve the same goal: legitimacy through association.

For national leaders, the rewards are immense. Football delivers soft power faster and cheaper than any public-relations firm ever could.

Fan Loyalty and Moral Dilemmas

For ordinary fans, the debate is personal. Can you support your team if you dislike its owners? Should politics matter in a sport built on passion?

Surveys show that most fans justify ownership changes pragmatically. They may object to human-rights records, but they also crave success after years of mediocrity. Football's emotional pull outweighs ethical discomfort. Winning feels like vindication, even when it comes at a moral cost.

At the same time, fan activism is growing. Supporter groups now campaign for ethical ownership rules, transparency in sponsorships, and fair financial play. Protests against Super League plans in 2021 proved that collective voices can still influence football's direction.

Yet it's difficult to protest against invisible power. Sovereign wealth funds don't answer to shareholders, and governments rarely bow to fan petitions. The imbalance of influence remains staggering.

The Uncomfortable Truth

The rise of state-backed clubs has created one of football's greatest contradictions. On one hand, they've brought unprecedented professionalism, infrastructure, and talent to the sport. On the other, they've blurred the line between competition and politics, between sport and strategy.

When a goal is scored at the Etihad, Parc des Princes, or St. James' Park, it's celebrated as sport—but also functions as branding. Every victory tells a story about the nation behind the team.

This doesn't mean fans are complicit in propaganda, but it does mean football is no longer politically neutral. Every chant, broadcast, and headline participates in a wider narrative shaped by money and power.

Between Passion and Power

As the game grows richer, its dependence on state wealth deepens. UEFA and FIFA rely on sponsorships and tournament bids from Gulf states. European clubs depend on petro-money to stay competitive. Journalists depend on access funded by those same sponsors.

The result is an ecosystem where criticizing the system feels almost impossible. Yet, paradoxically, the sport still inspires pure emotion. The love that fans feel—the heartbreak, the thrill, the loyalty—remains untouched.

Football's beauty endures precisely because it exists in tension: between people and power, between joy and politics, between what it means to win and what it costs.

That tension defines the modern era of the game. The question is whether football can continue to thrive under it—or whether, one day, the business of nations will consume the game entirely.

As the next chapter reveals, state-backed ownership didn't just change clubs; it birthed an empire. From Manchester to Melbourne, from Paris to New York, football became a global franchise machine, where billionaires and governments no longer compete for trophies alone—they compete for territory.

Chapter 5 – The New Football Empire

From City to the World

In 2014, football fans scrolling through their news feeds noticed something strange. Manchester City had just bought another club—**New York City FC**, a new franchise set to play in Major League Soccer. Within a year, another appeared in Australia: **Melbourne City FC**. Soon there were teams in Spain, Uruguay, China, Japan, India, and even Italy.

The idea seemed impossible at first. Why would one organization own clubs on five continents? But for Abu Dhabi's **City Football Group (CFG)**, the logic was clear. This wasn't just sport—it was **empire building**.

CFG wasn't content with one team; it wanted a **football network**, a global ecosystem of clubs sharing data, talent, branding, and management philosophies. Manchester City would be the crown jewel, and every satellite club would feed into it.

What began as a single-state project in Manchester had become something larger: a new model of globalization within football—where ownership stretched beyond borders, and identity became a strategic asset.

Multi-Club Ownership: The Next Frontier

The City Football Group's success inspired imitation. Other investors realized that multi-club ownership offered several unique advantages: talent development pipelines, risk diversification, and access to multiple markets at once.

Red Bull had already pioneered the concept years earlier, transforming **Austria's SV Salzburg** and **Germany's RB Leipzig** into high-energy, data-driven football machines. American investment groups such as **777 Partners**, **Eagle Football Holdings**, and **V Sports (Aston Villa's parent company)** began acquiring stakes in clubs across Europe, South America, and Africa.

The idea was straightforward: replicate corporate synergy in sport. A player developed in Uruguay could be loaned to Spain for experience, then sold to England for profit. Scouting networks could share information, commercial departments could pool sponsors, and digital teams could coordinate global fan engagement.

In short, multi-club ownership turned football into a **vertical supply chain**—from grassroots to global stage.

The Franchise Logic

Traditional football culture values local identity. Clubs represent cities, not corporations. But the new empire model treats clubs like **brands in a portfolio**. They're linked not by geography or history, but by ownership and operational efficiency.

To modern investors, this approach makes perfect sense. It spreads financial risk, improves economies of scale, and gives global sponsors a unified platform. But to fans, it often feels like a takeover of the sport's soul.

Red Bull's complete rebranding of **RB Leipzig** is the clearest example. The club's name, colors, and badge were redesigned to match the energy drink's logo. Its rise through Germany's divisions was meteoric—but controversial. Critics accused Red Bull of destroying tradition and turning football into marketing. Yet, for younger audiences raised in a corporate world, Leipzig's sleek professionalism felt natural.

City Football Group took a softer approach. Each team kept a local identity but shared City's sky-blue color palette, management philosophy, and digital strategy. What used to be a neighborhood club was now part of a multinational organization run from Abu Dhabi and London.

The Rise of Data Empires

Beneath the glossy branding lies another revolution: **data**.

Modern multi-club networks operate like tech companies. Every training session, pass, sprint, and heartbeat is recorded, analyzed, and fed into central databases. CFG employs data scientists to track performance across continents. Red Bull uses predictive modeling to identify talent before rivals do.

Analytics no longer support decisions—they drive them. Algorithms recommend signings, forecast injuries, and determine when to sell players for peak value. Football's romantic notion of "gut instinct" scouting has been replaced by machine learning.

Investors love it. Data means efficiency, and efficiency means profit. But it also strips away some of the sport's unpredictability. When clubs start optimizing everything from recruitment to tactics, matches can feel less human, more algorithmic.

Global Brands, Local Shadows

Multi-club ownership has turned football into a borderless industry. Yet that globalization comes with trade-offs.

In New York, fans often complain that **NYCFC** feels like Manchester City's little brother rather than a true American club. In Melbourne, some supporters resent being part of a corporate chain. Even Girona in Spain—a CFG-owned club that recently achieved stunning success in La Liga—is seen by rivals as a satellite, not an independent competitor.

The same pattern repeats across the world: new money brings success but erodes uniqueness. Local rivalries fade when ownership blurs identities. Community traditions are replaced by brand guidelines.

For many fans, that's the tragedy of the new football empire—it wins games but loses meaning.

The Financial Web

From a financial perspective, the empire model is revolutionary. By owning multiple clubs, investors can **control the entire player lifecycle**. Instead of relying on transfer markets, they move players internally, reducing costs and generating consistent revenue streams.

A young player bought cheaply in South America can be tested in Europe without risking major transfer fees. If he succeeds, he's sold for profit; if not, he's recycled within the network.

Meanwhile, sponsorship deals can be negotiated globally. Etihad Airways sponsors several City Football Group clubs simultaneously. Red Bull's branding stretches seamlessly from Salzburg to Leipzig to New York. This global leverage attracts advertisers and reduces costs, giving multi-club owners a decisive commercial edge over traditional clubs.

But critics worry this creates monopolies. When one company controls multiple teams across leagues, conflicts of interest arise—especially when those teams might face each other in continental competitions.

UEFA's Dilemma

UEFA and domestic federations have struggled to regulate this phenomenon. In theory, two clubs under the same ownership cannot play in the same European competition. In practice, it's far murkier.

When **RB Leipzig** and **Red Bull Salzburg** both qualified for the Champions League, UEFA approved participation after Red Bull made "structural adjustments" to claim the clubs were independently managed. Few believed it.

Similarly, as more CFG teams climb their national leagues, the possibility of internal conflicts increases. Critics argue that such arrangements undermine the spirit of fair competition. How can football remain credible if opponents share owners, sponsors, or even scouting data?

Yet UEFA faces a dilemma. Multi-club groups bring stability, professionalism, and massive investment to struggling teams. Banning them outright would risk financial collapse for smaller clubs that depend on these investors.

The American Invasion

Behind this trend is a wave of **American capital**. U.S. investors see European football as an undervalued asset class—comparable to owning a Hollywood studio or streaming platform.

Private-equity firms such as **Clearlake Capital (Chelsea)**, **777 Partners**, and **RedBird Capital (AC Milan)** don't view clubs as isolated entities but as content engines. Matches are episodes, seasons are story arcs, and fans are global subscribers.

To them, the goal isn't just winning trophies—it's **scaling the product**. That means global merchandising, international preseason tours, and streaming partnerships.

This "portfolio mindset" treats football like venture capital: buy low, optimize operations, grow brand value, and eventually sell high. For purists, it's blasphemy. For financiers, it's genius.

The Corporate Pyramid

What's emerging is a new kind of football hierarchy. At the top sit mega-groups like City Football Group and Red Bull—modern empires spanning continents. Below them are regional networks owned by private funds, each looking to feed players and profits upward.

Independent clubs—those still owned by communities or individuals—struggle to compete. Their budgets are smaller, their reach limited, their sponsors local. In an age of data-driven globalization, sentimentality is a disadvantage.

Football, once a patchwork of national cultures, is evolving into a consolidated industry. Instead of rivalry between nations, we now see rivalry between conglomerates.

Innovation or Colonization?

Supporters and analysts are divided on whether this evolution is progress or peril.

Optimists point to professional management, long-term investment, and access to technology that small clubs could never afford on their own. Multi-club networks can stabilize finances and give young players global exposure.

Skeptics see cultural colonization. The same corporations that dominate streaming, tech, and finance now dominate football. What began as a sport of local pride has become a sandbox for global elites.

Even club slogans reflect the change. "Cityzens of the World" or "One Red Bull Philosophy" sound less like football mottos and more like corporate mission statements.

The Fan Response

Fan reactions range from pragmatic acceptance to outright resistance. Some supporters appreciate the professionalism and success new ownership brings. Others feel alienated by the homogenization of their clubs.

In 2023, a coalition of fan groups from across Europe launched the **Against Multi-Club Ownership campaign,** calling for stricter UEFA rules and public transparency. Their argument was simple: a sport that belongs to everyone cannot be controlled by a handful of global investors.

But power rarely flows backward. As long as multi-club models deliver profit, they will expand. And for every fan who protests, millions more across emerging markets are joining the audience—fans who don't care who owns their team, as long as the football is good.

The New Football Map

The modern map of football isn't drawn by borders—it's drawn by ownership lines.

- City Football Group spans 13 clubs across five continents.

- Red Bull operates teams in Austria, Germany, the U.S., and Brazil.

- 777 Partners and Eagle Football hold stakes across Europe.

- American funds own more than half of Premier League clubs.

Each network functions like a mini-empire, complete with its own culture, strategy, and propaganda. Together, they've created a world where competition and collaboration intertwine—rivals on the pitch, partners off it.

The Takeaway

Football's latest transformation isn't about billionaires anymore—it's about systems.

The age of individual tycoons has given way to the age of corporate empires. The sport is now shaped by data scientists, investment managers, and brand architects who may never watch a match in person.

The question haunting fans and regulators alike is simple: **Can football remain a game when it's run like an algorithm?**

As this empire expands, smaller clubs face extinction, while global ones grow ever more alike. The charm of local rivalry and the unpredictability of competition are fading into a world optimized for efficiency.

But history shows that empires, no matter how vast, eventually meet resistance. And as football's next chapter unfolds, that resistance will come not from governments or corporations—but from the people who refuse to let the world's game become just another business.

Chapter 6 – How Clubs Became Brands

The Moment Football Went Mainstream

It wasn't a goal, a trophy, or a transfer that changed football's commercial destiny. It was a photo shoot. In 1997, **David Beckham** appeared in a sharp Armani suit, smiling for the cameras in a London department store. He wasn't selling shirts or tickets—he was selling style.

That image marked the moment football stepped fully into the world of pop culture. Beckham wasn't just a Manchester United midfielder; he was a global brand. Within a few years, he had sponsorships with Adidas, Pepsi, and Gillette. His marriage to Spice Girl Victoria Adams turned him into a household name from London to Los Angeles.

For Manchester United, this was priceless. Every Beckham photo, every magazine cover, every advert carried the club's logo in the background. Suddenly, footballers weren't just athletes—they were marketing assets. And clubs weren't just sports teams—they were lifestyle brands.

The Shift from Club to Corporation

By the early 2000s, clubs had realized they could no longer rely solely on matchday revenue or TV rights. To compete globally, they needed to build *brand ecosystems*.

Manchester United led the charge. Under CEO **Peter Kenyon** and later **David Gill**, the club launched regional offices in Asia and the U.S., developed merchandising deals in dozens of countries, and turned preseason tours into promotional roadshows.

Liverpool followed with "This Means More," a global marketing campaign that sold emotion as much as football. Arsenal emphasized "The Arsenal Way," a blend of heritage and class. Meanwhile, Real Madrid trademarked **Los Galácticos**, turning its superstars—Zidane, Ronaldo, Figo, Beckham—into a commercial machine.

The logic was simple: the club crest was no longer just a symbol—it was an **asset**.

The Economics of Emotion

Branding in football depends on a simple equation: loyalty equals lifetime value.

Every fan who buys a jersey, streams highlights, or subscribes to club content is a customer. The goal is to convert emotion into economics. Clubs now employ data analysts and marketing strategists who track engagement metrics, merchandise sales, and regional fan behavior.

A modern football club resembles a hybrid of Netflix, Nike, and Apple—producing content, selling products, and nurturing user loyalty. The sport's emotional foundation makes it uniquely profitable; once someone identifies as a fan, they rarely switch allegiance.

That kind of customer retention is every marketer's dream.

From Terraces to Timelines

The rise of social media accelerated the shift. Platforms like Twitter, Instagram, and TikTok turned football into a 24/7 conversation.

No longer did clubs communicate only on matchdays. Now they posted training clips, birthday messages, memes, and behind-the-scenes content. Every interaction reinforced brand personality.

Manchester City positioned itself as the sleek, tech-savvy innovator. Liverpool framed itself as emotional and community-driven. PSG leaned into fashion and celebrity culture, blurring the lines between sport and luxury.

A club's tone of voice, color palette, and social-media strategy became as important as its tactics on the pitch. Fans no longer waited for highlights—they consumed football like a lifestyle feed.

The Star System

Superstar players became walking billboards. Clubs realized that signing a global icon could multiply their reach overnight.

When **Cristiano Ronaldo** returned to Manchester United in 2021, the club's share price briefly spiked by 9 percent, and the team gained 10 million new social followers within a week. Similarly, **Lionel Messi's** move to PSG in 2021 brought the club a massive boost in merchandise sales and global exposure.

These weren't just football transfers—they were brand mergers. Each star brought a loyal online audience, often bigger than the clubs themselves. Ronaldo, for instance, has more followers than all Premier League teams combined.

For clubs, players became marketing partners as much as athletes. Sponsorship contracts were now built around *image rights*, and every goal doubled as a marketing event.

The Merchandise Empire

Walk through any major city—from Jakarta to Johannesburg—and you'll find football shirts everywhere. Jerseys have become both fashion and identity.

In the 1990s, shirt sponsorship was simple: one logo, one deal. Today, clubs run multi-layered sponsorship models. There's a main shirt sponsor, a sleeve sponsor, a training-kit sponsor, and even an official airline, car, and cryptocurrency partner.

Each space on a player's kit is a marketing opportunity worth millions. The **Premier League's global audience of 4.7 billion** viewers ensures that any logo displayed there reaches every corner of the world.

Meanwhile, merchandise has evolved beyond jerseys. Clubs sell retro collections, phone cases, fragrances, NFTs, and even coffee. Barcelona's official store on Las Ramblas looks more like an Apple flagship than a sports shop.

The football industry no longer sells results—it sells belonging.

The Netflix Effect

Another major shift came with football's entry into streaming entertainment.

Clubs and leagues realized that fans wanted not just matches, but *stories*. Behind-the-scenes documentaries like **Amazon's All or Nothing** (featuring Manchester City, Tottenham, and Arsenal) and Netflix's **Sunderland 'Til I Die** turned football into episodic drama.

These shows humanized players, revealed dressing-room tension, and deepened fan connection. For clubs, they were marketing gold: every tear, speech, and training montage strengthened brand identity.

Even smaller clubs jumped on the trend. Wrexham AFC, bought by Hollywood actors Ryan Reynolds and Rob McElhenney, leveraged storytelling to transform from a forgotten Welsh team into a global phenomenon. Their docuseries attracted millions of viewers and new sponsors—proof that narrative could rival trophies in financial impact.

From Loyalty to Lifestyle

The modern fan isn't just a supporter—they're a lifestyle consumer.

Clubs now sell experiences that extend far beyond the pitch: stadium tours, subscription apps, esports teams, branded hotels, and even financial services.

Barcelona launched **Barça Studios** to produce original content and explore digital ventures. Real Madrid's **RM Play** offers premium video access. Manchester United partnered with tech firms to launch virtual reality experiences.

Football is evolving from sport to **entertainment ecosystem**, blending technology, storytelling, and commerce.

This transformation isn't accidental—it's strategic. By embedding themselves into fans' daily lives, clubs ensure constant engagement. Every tweet, clip, or purchase reinforces the emotional bond.

The Dark Side of Branding

But there's a cost to all this polish.

As clubs chase global markets, they risk losing their local roots. Ticket prices climb to fund stadium renovations and global campaigns. Traditional fans are replaced by tourists eager to post selfies. The roar of the terraces gives way to the hum of phone cameras.

Critics argue that football's authenticity is being packaged and sold back to the very people who created it. When a club rebrands its logo, changes its anthem, or adjusts kickoff times for Asian audiences, it chips away at its heritage.

In this new landscape, "support" has become "engagement," and loyalty has been redefined as "customer retention."

The Case Studies

Manchester United remains the archetype—a club that mastered branding before branding became fashionable. Its global academy of fans in Asia and Africa ensures steady merchandise sales even in trophy droughts.

Barcelona turned "More Than a Club" (*Més que un club*) into a political and emotional identity, blending Catalan pride with modern marketing. Yet its commercial overreach led to crippling debt, showing that branding without balance can backfire.

PSG, under Qatari ownership, perfected luxury football marketing. Collaborations with Dior, Jordan Brand, and Balmain elevated it from sports team to fashion label. Even the club's Instagram looks like a designer catalog.

Each example reveals a truth: modern success depends as much on cultural relevance as on sporting excellence.

The Metrics of Fame

A generation ago, a club's worth was measured in trophies. Today, it's measured in metrics: engagement rates, follower counts, and brand equity.

Executives track *share of voice*—how often their club dominates global headlines. Social-media analytics dictate content strategies. Matchday programs have been replaced by TikTok trends.

This obsession with visibility has made football indistinguishable from entertainment media. Clubs compete not just against each other but against Netflix, YouTube, and Fortnite for audience attention.

When Clubs Outgrow Football

The world's biggest clubs have transcended sport entirely. They now operate as **cultural brands**, shaping music, fashion, and online identity. Collaborations between teams and pop icons—Drake with Barcelona, Jay-Z with Arsenal, BTS with Tottenham—blur the line between fandom and culture.

For younger audiences, football is as much about lifestyle as results. Wearing a PSG jersey in Seoul or Los Angeles isn't about supporting the team—it's about belonging to a global aesthetic.

This universality gives clubs immense power. But it also makes them vulnerable. If a club's identity is built on trend rather than tradition, what happens when the trend fades?

The Takeaway

The evolution of football into a brand-driven industry has made it richer, louder, and more global than ever. But it's also raised a question that no marketing department can answer: *can a club sell authenticity once it's been commercialized?*

Football's brand boom has blurred lines between sport, business, and culture. It has created billion-dollar empires and global icons—but it has also tested the soul of the game.

As we'll see in the next chapter, this clash between money and meaning would soon explode into open rebellion. Fans who once cheered the rise of global football would take to the streets to defend it—when the richest clubs on Earth tried to form a league of their own.

Chapter 7 – The Fans vs. the Money

The Day the Fans Fought Back

It was supposed to be an ordinary Sunday in April 2021. Instead, it became one of the most explosive days in modern football history.

Outside **Old Trafford**, thousands of Manchester United supporters gathered, waving green-and-gold scarves—the colors of the club's founders before the Glazers took control. They sang, chanted, and finally broke through security barriers, storming the pitch. Flares burned in the stands. Banners read *"Created by the poor, stolen by the rich."*

Their anger wasn't just about ownership or debt. It was about betrayal. The night before, news had leaked that twelve of Europe's biggest clubs—including Manchester United, Liverpool, Arsenal, Chelsea, Manchester City, Real Madrid, and Juventus—had secretly agreed to form a **European Super League (ESL)**.

It was meant to be the ultimate elite competition: permanent membership for the richest clubs, guaranteed broadcast revenue, and total independence from UEFA. To its backers, it was progress. To fans, it was sacrilege.

Within forty-eight hours, football's power balance shifted—not through money or politics, but through people. Fans organized protests across Europe, forcing clubs to withdraw. What began as an act of corporate dominance ended as a reminder that, for all its wealth, football still belonged to the crowd.

The Shrinking Voice of the Supporter

For most of football's history, fans weren't customers—they were *stakeholders*.

In England, local supporters founded clubs, built stadiums, and ran committees. Tickets were cheap enough for anyone to attend. The connection between club and community was direct, even personal.

But from the 1990s onward, as TV money poured in, that relationship began to erode. Clubs became corporations. Ticket prices rose. Stadiums turned into entertainment venues. The matchday experience—once noisy, local, and unpredictable—became a sanitized product designed for broadcast appeal.

Fans didn't disappear; they were simply reclassified. Their loyalty was monetized through merchandise, memberships, and subscriptions. The voice that once echoed through stands now echoed online, often ignored by those in charge.

The Super League announcement was the breaking point—a moment when decades of resentment boiled over.

When Passion Meets Profit

At its core, the fans-versus-money conflict is emotional. Supporters see clubs as cultural institutions—extensions of family, neighborhood, and identity. Owners see them as assets.

The **Glazer family's** leveraged buyout of Manchester United in 2005 epitomized this clash. The takeover saddled the club with hundreds of millions in debt, sparking mass protests and the formation of a breakaway team, **FC United of Manchester**, owned entirely by fans.

Liverpool faced similar unrest in 2016 when owners **Fenway Sports Group** announced a ticket-price increase to £77. Midway through a match against Sunderland, thousands of fans walked out in protest. The message worked—the club quickly reversed its decision.

These moments exposed a deeper truth: money could buy stadiums and players, but it couldn't buy legitimacy.

The German Exception

If England represents the commercialization of football, **Germany** represents its resistance.

The **50+1 rule**, which ensures that club members (usually fans) retain majority voting rights, has protected German football from corporate control. While exceptions exist—such as Bayer Leverkusen and Wolfsburg, both owned by corporations—the majority of Bundesliga clubs remain community-oriented.

This system has kept ticket prices affordable and fan culture vibrant. Stadiums like Dortmund's **Yellow Wall** prove that atmosphere and authenticity can coexist with modern success.

During the Super League scandal, German clubs like **Bayern Munich** and **Borussia Dortmund** refused to join, citing fan ownership as the reason. Their loyalty to supporters made them heroes in a moment of global outrage.

The contrast was stark: in England, fans protested outside; in Germany, they already sat inside the boardroom.

The Digital Megaphone

The rise of social media gave fans a weapon more powerful than banners: visibility.

Within hours of the Super League announcement, hashtags like **#NoToSuperLeague** and **#FootballForTheFans** trended worldwide. Supporters from rival clubs united in outrage. Politicians weighed in. Even players spoke out.

Liverpool captain **Jordan Henderson** tweeted on behalf of his squad: *"We don't like it and we don't want it to happen."* Manchester City manager **Pep Guardiola** called the idea "not sport when success is guaranteed." The digital backlash was overwhelming.

Under relentless pressure, one club after another withdrew from the project. The entire league collapsed in two days—a billion-dollar idea undone by public fury.

It was a watershed moment. For the first time in decades, fans realized they could still change football's direction.

The Price of Progress

Even with those victories, the tide of commercialization hasn't stopped.

Ticket prices in the Premier League remain among the highest in Europe. Clubs continue to push luxury seating, global marketing, and exclusive content subscriptions. The gap between those who watch from the stands and those who watch from streaming platforms widens every year.

Football's new business model values global reach over local connection. A fan in Shanghai or Chicago may matter more financially than one in Sheffield or Sunderland. The community that built the game often feels like an afterthought.

The irony is painful: the more global football becomes, the more alienated its traditional fans feel.

When Clubs Forget Their Roots

Few moments capture this better than when **Cardiff City**, under Malaysian owner Vincent Tan, changed its home colors from blue to red in 2012 to appeal to Asian markets. Fans revolted. After three years of unrest, the club restored its original blue.

A similar story unfolded in Hull City, where owner Assem Allam tried to rebrand the team as "Hull Tigers" to attract international investors. Fans protested until the plan was dropped.

These examples reveal the limits of commercialization. When branding decisions override heritage, supporters fight back. And when they do, global PR collapses faster than any financial forecast.

Football as Cultural Resistance

For many fans, supporting their club has become an act of resistance—a statement that football's soul can't be entirely bought.

Grassroots movements like **Supporters Direct** in the UK and **Football Supporters Europe** advocate for fan representation in ownership and governance. Some groups have even reclaimed clubs. **AFC Wimbledon**, founded in 2002 after the original Wimbledon FC relocated and became MK Dons, is entirely fan-owned and community-run.

These stories may not make global headlines, but they represent something powerful: proof that football's democratic spirit still flickers beneath the corporate surface.

The Paradox of the Modern Fan

Yet modern fans live a contradiction. They decry commercialization while consuming it daily—buying jerseys, subscribing to club content, and posting highlights online. Every click reinforces the same economy they criticize.

It's not hypocrisy; it's helplessness. Football has become so global, so financially dependent on commercialization, that opting out feels impossible. The matchday ticket may be optional, but the emotional investment is not.

Even the most vocal critics admit that when the whistle blows and the team scores, business fades into the background. That's football's enduring power—it transcends the very system that exploits it.

The Return of the Crowd

Despite everything, fans remain the heartbeat of the sport. Without them, football's billion-dollar ecosystem collapses. Broadcasters need atmosphere, sponsors need loyalty, and players need an audience.

That's why, after the Super League debacle, clubs rushed to repair relationships. Executives issued apologies. Community initiatives multiplied. The message was clear: you can own the club, but not its meaning.

In 2023, Manchester United even invited fan representatives to board meetings—a symbolic gesture, perhaps, but one that signaled renewed awareness. The lesson of 2021 lingered: ignore supporters, and the game itself revolts.

The Takeaway

The battle between fans and money isn't over—it's only evolving.

Supporters may not own the stadiums or the TV networks, but they still own something more powerful: legitimacy. Every chant, every protest, every refusal to accept football as mere content keeps the sport alive.

The Super League collapse proved that billionaires could buy clubs, but not culture. That the world's game, for all its greed, still beats with a human heart.

Yet as football's global economy continues to expand, new pressures loom—digital transformation, new investors, and the blurred lines between sport, media, and technology.

In the next chapter, we'll see how those forces collided during the biggest power grab in modern football history: the rise and fall of the **European Super League** itself—where money, politics, and rebellion met head-on.

Chapter 8 – The European Super League Fiasco

The Midnight Coup

It began on a Sunday night in April 2021, while most fans were asleep. A joint press release—cold, corporate, and quietly seismic—hit inboxes across Europe.

"Twelve leading European football clubs have today come together to announce the formation of a new competition, the European Super League."

Within minutes, the names spread across social media like wildfire: **Manchester United, Liverpool, Manchester City, Chelsea, Arsenal, Tottenham, Real Madrid, Barcelona, Atlético Madrid, Juventus, Inter Milan, and AC Milan.**

The timing was deliberate—midnight in Europe, Sunday evening in the United States. The announcement blindsided UEFA, national associations, and even players. The **Super League** wasn't a rumor anymore. It was a reality—one that threatened to blow up a century of football tradition.

The project's architect, **Florentino Pérez**, President of Real Madrid, framed it as salvation. "Young people are no longer interested in football," he claimed. "We need to make it more attractive." Behind the PR gloss was a simpler motive: money.

The COVID-19 pandemic had battered club finances. Real Madrid and Barcelona were drowning in debt; English giants had lost hundreds of millions in matchday revenue. The Super League promised guaranteed income—no relegation, no uncertainty, no UEFA oversight.

To its creators, it was evolution. To everyone else, it was betrayal.

The Architects of a Revolt

At the heart of the plan stood a small circle of billionaires and executives.

Florentino Pérez saw it as the natural progression of elite football—a self-contained league modeled on American sports franchises. **Andrea Agnelli**, then president of Juventus and chairman of the European Club Association (ECA), quietly turned on UEFA, betraying his allies to join the project. **Joel Glazer** of Manchester United and **Stan Kroenke** of Arsenal saw an opportunity to import the U.S. franchise model to Europe, locking in profits and removing risk.

For them, the current system was inefficient. Why should Manchester United or Real Madrid, with global audiences of hundreds of millions, share revenue with smaller clubs? Why risk missing the Champions League, where the real money was made?

The Super League promised each founding member over **€300 million in entry payments**, with annual revenues exceeding anything UEFA could offer. Backed by **JP Morgan Chase**, the plan was financially bulletproof—on paper.

But its creators made one fatal mistake: they underestimated emotion.

The Business Logic

To understand why so many powerful owners supported the project, it helps to see it through their eyes.

The Champions League, once football's crown jewel, had become unpredictable. Clubs with massive wage bills risked elimination after one bad night. Domestic leagues were also losing value; in some countries, the same clubs won every year.

In boardrooms, football looked broken. The Super League offered a **closed competition** with permanent membership for its founding teams—similar to the NBA or NFL. That meant stable revenues, guaranteed global viewership, and more control over commercial rights.

In short, it replaced sporting jeopardy with financial certainty.

It was, however, a system designed by accountants, not athletes. The beauty of football lies in its openness—where Leicester City can win the Premier League and a fourth-division club can dream of Wembley. By eliminating risk, the Super League eliminated hope.

The Global Backlash

The reaction was instant and ferocious.

Within hours, **Gary Neville**, the former Manchester United captain turned pundit, delivered an on-air tirade on Sky Sports:

> "It's an absolute disgrace. They're stealing the game from the people who love it. Deduct points, relegate them, do whatever it takes."

His outrage captured the mood of millions. Fans took to the streets. Outside **Stamford Bridge**, Chelsea supporters blocked the team bus before a match, forcing the club to publicly reconsider its decision. Protesters waved banners reading *"R.I.P. Football"* and *"Fans Before Finance."*

Politicians weighed in. UK Prime Minister **Boris Johnson** threatened legislative action to block the plan. **Prince William**, president of the English FA, condemned it. Even UEFA president **Aleksander Čeferin**—normally measured—called it "a spit in the face of football lovers."

The backlash wasn't limited to Europe. In Asia, Africa, and South America, fans expressed disbelief that their beloved clubs would lock themselves into an elite cartel.

Social media amplified every voice. Hashtags like **#NoToSuperLeague** trended worldwide. Memes mocked billionaire owners who didn't understand the game they owned. Within 48 hours, the global audience united against the very institutions that claimed to represent it.

The Collapse

The first domino fell on April 20. Under pressure from fans and government officials, **Chelsea** announced it would withdraw. Manchester City followed hours later. By the next morning, all six English clubs had pulled out.

Without England's backbone, the entire project collapsed. Juventus, Milan, and Atlético backed away. Even Barcelona—still drowning in debt—hesitated. Only Real Madrid and a defiant Florentino Pérez refused to concede defeat.

What had taken years of secret planning crumbled in less than two days.

The humiliation was total. Pérez's dream of a billionaire utopia had become a global laughingstock. Agnelli resigned from the European Club Association. Joel Glazer was forced to issue a public apology to Manchester United fans, admitting he had "got it wrong."

The project's death was as swift as its birth—and its lesson was unmistakable.

A Sport, Not a Stock Market

The Super League fiasco exposed the growing disconnect between football's boardrooms and its base.

To the billionaires who run elite clubs, football is an entertainment product. To fans, it's an inheritance. The owners saw numbers; supporters saw memories. The two realities collided, and for once, the balance tipped toward the people.

But the story also revealed how fragile that balance is. The same forces that birthed the Super League—debt, inequality, and greed—still shape modern football. The collapse didn't fix the system; it only delayed its evolution.

UEFA's Countermove

In the aftermath, UEFA rushed to restore control. They restructured the **Champions League format**, expanding the number of teams and matches to increase revenue. Critics called it "the Super League in disguise."

Meanwhile, FIFA used the chaos to push its own ambitions: a revamped **Club World Cup** with more teams, more sponsors, and more global reach. The irony wasn't lost on fans—those who condemned the Super League were quietly pursuing similar goals.

The difference lay in presentation. UEFA and FIFA framed their expansions as inclusive, even though they served the same economic logic: more games, more money, more control.

Super League 2.0

The idea of a breakaway competition didn't die—it evolved.

In 2022, a company called **A22 Sports Management** revived the project with a new proposal: an open, merit-based European league system with promotion and relegation. They claimed it would be fairer, sustainable, and fan-friendly.

Real Madrid, Barcelona, and Juventus remained loyal to the cause, arguing that UEFA held an illegal monopoly. The case went all the way to the **European Court of Justice**, where the legal battle continues to this day.

Though the rebrand softened the rhetoric, the core motive remained the same—clubs wanted control over their own destiny, free from UEFA's regulations. Whether the plan ever materializes again is uncertain, but the ambition behind it never truly disappeared.

What the Fiasco Revealed

The Super League collapse became a mirror for football's soul.

It revealed that fans still hold moral authority, even in an age of billionaires and sovereign wealth. It showed that players and managers, once silent employees, can sway public opinion. And it reminded everyone—from boardrooms to broadcasters—that football's strength lies not in ownership, but in *community*.

Yet it also exposed the sport's hypocrisy. Many of the same fans who condemned the Super League still watch clubs owned by oil states and hedge funds. Many pundits who called for reform work for broadcasters that helped inflate football's financial bubble.

The line between protector and profiteer remains thin.

The Takeaway

The European Super League wasn't just a failed business plan—it was a symptom of football's deeper sickness: the belief that more money automatically means progress.

In trying to privatize passion, the architects of the Super League underestimated what makes the game special. Football isn't designed to be efficient; it's designed to be unpredictable, unfair, and gloriously human.

For forty-eight hours in April 2021, the world saw what football would look like without that humanity—and collectively said no.

But the fight for football's soul isn't over. The same financial pressures that birthed the Super League are still rising. As global investors, digital platforms, and private equity funds flood the game, the next battle will be even bigger.

Because if billionaires couldn't buy football outright, they'll simply build a new version of it—from the inside out.

Chapter 9 – American Money in Football

The Takeover That Changed Everything

When **Malcolm Glazer** bought **Manchester United** in 2005, the deal wasn't greeted with champagne—it was met with fury.

Fans gathered outside Old Trafford carrying placards reading *"Love United, Hate Glazer."* They weren't angry because an outsider had bought their club; they were angry because of **how** he bought it.

Glazer used a **leveraged buyout (LBO)**—a financial maneuver common in American corporate takeovers but unheard of in football. He borrowed hundreds of millions of pounds to purchase United, using the club's own assets as collateral. In short, Manchester United paid for its own sale.

For a sport built on loyalty and local pride, this was corporate heresy. The club that once prided itself on belonging to the people of Manchester was now a heavily indebted business owned by a Florida billionaire.

The Glazers' move marked the start of a new era: the **American invasion** of European football.

The Franchise Mindset

To understand U.S. investors in football, you have to understand the **American sports model**.

In the U.S., professional leagues like the NFL, NBA, and MLB operate as **closed franchises**. There's no promotion or relegation. Owners buy a license to operate a team in a guaranteed market. Profits are shared, costs are capped, and risk is limited.

For decades, European football was the opposite—open, merit-based, and chaotic. Clubs rose and fell on results, not balance sheets. But to American investors, that chaos looked like inefficiency.

They saw untapped potential: global fanbases, weak financial regulations, and historic brands that hadn't yet been fully monetized. Football, in their eyes, wasn't a pastime—it was **undervalued intellectual property**.

Why Europe Looked Like a Bargain

By the late 2010s, America's billionaires had already transformed their domestic sports into billion-dollar entertainment machines. Stadiums became event spaces. Players became influencers. Every inch of real estate—from jerseys to app screens—was monetized.

When they looked across the Atlantic, European football appeared ripe for the same treatment.

Take **Liverpool**. When **Fenway Sports Group (FSG)** bought the club in 2010 for around £300 million, it was struggling on and off the pitch. Within a decade, FSG had turned it into a global powerhouse worth over **£4 billion**—through disciplined spending, data-driven recruitment, and world-class marketing.

Stan Kroenke, already owner of multiple U.S. franchises, applied the same long-term commercial logic to **Arsenal**, emphasizing real estate, media rights, and global branding over short-term spending.

For **Todd Boehly** and **Clearlake Capital**, who bought **Chelsea** in 2022 for £4.25 billion, the appeal wasn't just football—it was content. As Boehly told investors, "We think the Premier League is incredibly undervalued compared to U.S. sports."

The Business Playbook

American investors don't buy clubs for love; they buy them for **scalability**. Their approach follows a predictable pattern:

1. **Monetize assets** – Stadium naming rights, ticket tiers, VIP experiences.

2. **Optimize costs** – Use analytics to evaluate performance and recruitment efficiency.

3. **Diversify revenue** – Merchandising, international tours, streaming deals, esports, and digital collectibles.

4. **Expand reach** – Build global fanbases in Asia, Africa, and the U.S. through marketing campaigns and academies.

They bring financial discipline—but also corporate detachment. Decisions are made by committees and spreadsheets, not by gut or tradition. The club becomes a "brand platform," not a civic institution.

The Data Revolution

Much of the American takeover mentality stems from the **Moneyball era**—the idea that data analytics can outthink intuition.

In baseball, the concept revolutionized team building. In football, it's done the same. FSG's Liverpool famously used data to identify undervalued players like **Mohamed Salah** and **Andrew Robertson**—signings that powered their Premier League and Champions League triumphs.

Clubs under U.S. ownership now employ analytics departments rivaling those of Fortune 500 companies. Recruitment, injury prevention, and even fan engagement are optimized by algorithms.

It's efficient—but also clinical. Critics say this approach strips football of its soul, replacing artistry with metrics. For investors, though, data offers what passion never could: **predictable returns**.

The Cultural Clash

The Americanization of football hasn't come without friction.

European fans view clubs as heritage institutions, not entertainment franchises. They expect owners to respect history, rivalries, and local values. When American investors propose ideas like all-star games, closed leagues, or play-off formats, supporters recoil.

In 2022, **Todd Boehly** suggested a "North vs. South" Premier League all-star match to raise money for charity. Fans and pundits mocked the idea as tone-deaf, proof that he didn't understand football's culture.

To the American mind, such events are logical revenue boosters. To European supporters, they're commercial stunts that cheapen competition.

Private Equity Joins the Game

It's not just individuals anymore. The latest wave of American capital comes from **private equity funds**, which see football as a new asset class.

Firms like **777 Partners**, **RedBird Capital**, and **Silver Lake** invest in multiple clubs across different leagues, betting on long-term appreciation. RedBird owns stakes in **AC Milan**, **Toulouse**, and **Fenway Sports Group**. 777 Partners has built a portfolio spanning **Sevilla**, **Genoa**, and **Standard Liège**.

For these firms, football isn't about trophies—it's about **portfolio synergy**. Clubs are treated like subsidiaries, each contributing data, players, or media rights to a wider empire.

This approach mirrors venture capital logic: buy undervalued assets, optimize, scale, and sell. In a world where tech valuations have plateaued, football offers a new frontier of brand equity.

The Efficiency Paradox

American investors have undeniably improved football's financial management. Many clubs now run sustainable operations after decades of reckless spending.

But efficiency has its price. The more football becomes a business, the less it feels like a sport. Clubs start to resemble content companies—efficient but interchangeable. Fans sense the difference. The passion feels rehearsed, the marketing relentless.

In trying to make football more predictable, investors risk killing the very chaos that makes it beautiful.

The American Dream Meets European Reality

Despite cultural resistance, the American presence is now too entrenched to reverse. As of 2025, **over half of Premier League clubs** are majority or partial U.S.-owned. American media companies hold major broadcasting rights. Even UEFA and FIFA now partner with U.S. sponsors and consultancies.

This isn't an invasion—it's integration. American capital and European tradition are merging into something new: **football as a global entertainment business**, run by executives who see no distinction between sports and streaming.

Yet the fundamental tension remains. Fans still measure success in silverware, not spreadsheets. The day a Champions League trophy is celebrated like a quarterly report will be the day football loses its soul.

Lessons from Across the Atlantic

Ironically, American owners often justify their approach by citing football's own flaws. They argue that European clubs historically mismanaged money, relied on emotional decision-making, and ignored global audiences.

And they're not wrong. Many traditional owners treated clubs like vanity projects, overspending for glory, then collapsing in debt. American investors, for all their corporate detachment, brought professionalism, long-term planning, and financial discipline.

But what they often miss is that football's magic comes *because* it defies logic. Fans don't fall in love with spreadsheets—they fall in love with stories. With nights that shouldn't have been possible. With underdogs who break the rules.

You can't monetize that without losing it.

The Takeaway

The rise of American money in football is both a rescue and a revolution. It's saved struggling clubs, professionalized management, and unlocked global audiences. But it's also turned heritage into inventory and fans into customers.

This is football's new frontier: efficient, global, and relentlessly monetized.

The American owners didn't conquer football—they **translated** it into their own language: franchises, analytics, and brand equity. Whether that translation enriches or erases the game's essence will depend on what comes next.

Because the next frontier isn't America or Europe—it's Asia. And as we'll see in the next chapter, the East has its own vision for football's future: one built not just on profit, but on power, prestige, and politics.

Chapter 10 – The Asian Expansion

The Golden Rush to the East

In 2016, headlines around the world declared that football had a new financial superpower—and it wasn't in Europe.

China's **Super League** was spending money like never before. Brazilian star **Oscar** left Chelsea for **Shanghai SIPG** in a deal worth £52 million. **Carlos Tevez** signed with **Shanghai Shenhua**, earning a reported £600,000 a week—making him, for a brief moment, the highest-paid player on earth. Even European coaches like **Sven-Göran Eriksson** and **Manuel Pellegrini** were lured east with contracts worth millions.

It was a stunning reversal of football's traditional power map. For decades, Asia had been the audience—never the stage. But suddenly, the world's best players were boarding flights to Shanghai, Guangzhou, and Beijing.

This was no accident. It was part of a broader political and economic project—China's attempt to use football as a symbol of its **national rise** and global ambition.

China's Football Dream

The spark came from the very top. In 2015, **President Xi Jinping**, a known football fan, unveiled a national plan to make China a "football powerhouse." The goals were bold: qualify for another World Cup, host one, and eventually win it.

The government poured billions into infrastructure, building thousands of pitches and academies. Corporations followed suit. Conglomerates like **Wanda Group, Evergrande**, and **Suning** invested heavily in clubs both domestic and international.

Wanda bought a stake in **Atlético Madrid**. Suning purchased **Inter Milan**. The message was clear: China was no longer content to just watch football—it wanted to own it.

For a few years, it worked. Crowds grew, TV rights soared, and global attention shifted east. But beneath the glitz, cracks were forming.

The Fall of the Chinese Super League

By 2020, the bubble had burst.

The Chinese government, facing debt crises and corruption scandals, imposed strict financial regulations. Clubs that had been spending recklessly were suddenly unable to pay wages.

Jiangsu FC, owned by Suning, won the league in 2020—and then folded just three months later. Stars like Oscar and Hulk returned to Brazil or Europe as the money dried up. Stadiums that had once symbolized ambition became monuments to overreach.

China's football dream hadn't died—it had simply collided with reality.

The lesson was clear: you can't buy football culture overnight. Passion takes generations to build, not transfer windows.

Japan's Long Game

While China's experiment imploded, **Japan** quietly demonstrated what a sustainable football revolution looks like.

Since launching the **J-League** in 1993, Japan has built one of the most stable, fan-focused football ecosystems in the world. Clubs are community-oriented, youth academies are robust, and matchday experiences rival Europe's best.

Japanese football's philosophy is patience over prestige. Instead of importing expensive foreign stars, the league invested in **local development**, producing players like **Shinji Kagawa**, **Keisuke Honda**, and **Takefusa Kubo**—who went on to succeed in Europe.

Corporate sponsors such as **Rakuten** (Barcelona's former shirt sponsor) and **Yanmar** tied the league's growth to Japan's technological and cultural exports. The result: a balanced, credible system admired across Asia.

Japan may never outspend Europe, but it has earned something far more valuable—respect and longevity.

South Korea's Steady Rise

Next door, **South Korea** followed a similar path, focusing on discipline, structure, and international success.

The **K-League**, established in 1983, laid the foundation for the country's footballing culture. But the real turning point came in **2002**, when South Korea co-hosted the **World Cup** and reached the semifinals.

That moment transformed football from a niche sport into a national obsession. Corporations like **Hyundai**, **Samsung**, and **LG** invested heavily in sponsorships and youth programs.

Two decades later, the country continues to produce global stars—**Son Heung-min**, **Kim Min-jae**, and **Lee Kang-in**—and export talent to Europe's biggest clubs.

Where China chased fame, Korea built fundamentals.

Southeast Asia: The Sleeping Giant

If Europe is the sport's heart and China its ambition, **Southeast Asia** is its passion.

From **Jakarta to Bangkok**, football dominates popular culture. The region's fan engagement numbers are staggering: Indonesia, Thailand, and Vietnam rank among the world's top countries for Premier League viewership.

European clubs have taken notice. Manchester United, Liverpool, and Barcelona routinely sell out 80,000-seat stadiums during preseason tours. Local broadcasters fight over streaming rights, and social media campaigns often target Southeast Asian fans specifically.

But despite its massive audiences, the region struggles with infrastructure, corruption, and inconsistent investment. Domestic leagues lack stability, and talented players often move abroad to develop.

Still, with a young population and deep emotional connection to the sport, Southeast Asia remains the biggest **untapped market** in world football.

The Business of Expansion

Football's eastward shift isn't just cultural—it's strategic.

Clubs and leagues know that Europe's markets are saturated. Asia, with its billions of potential consumers, offers limitless growth.

European clubs have opened academies across the continent:

- **Manchester City** in China, Singapore, and India.

- **Barcelona** in Japan and Indonesia.

- **Liverpool** in Thailand and South Korea.

Preseason tours have become marketing goldmines. A single friendly in Kuala Lumpur or Tokyo can generate millions in merchandise sales and sponsorships.

Meanwhile, Asian brands have become major global sponsors: **AIA** (Tottenham), **Yokohama Tyres** (Chelsea), **Rakuten** (Barcelona), **Emirates** (Arsenal and Real Madrid). The partnerships go both ways—Europe gets cash, Asia gets visibility.

The Clash Between Growth and Authenticity

But not everyone welcomes the expansion. Critics argue that clubs are prioritizing global markets over local fans. Match kickoff times are shifted for Asian TV audiences. Tours disrupt preseason preparation.

Some see the entire process as cultural imperialism—a one-way flow of Western influence under the guise of "development."

At the same time, Asian leagues face a reverse problem: imitation without identity. The Chinese Super League tried to copy Europe's glamour but neglected grassroots infrastructure. Smaller nations emulate Premier League branding instead of building unique local models.

The challenge for Asia is finding its **own voice** in global football—not as a consumer market, but as a genuine footballing power.

Women's Football and New Frontiers

One of Asia's most promising areas of growth lies in **women's football**.

Japan's national team won the **2011 Women's World Cup**, inspiring a generation. China's **Steel Roses** have regained prominence, and South Korea's women's league is expanding rapidly.

Brands see this as a new frontier: a fresh, inclusive image that aligns with modern marketing. European clubs like Arsenal and Chelsea now partner with Asian initiatives to develop women's academies.

It's a long-term play—but one with enormous potential.

Lessons from the East

Asia's story is both an inspiration and a warning.

China proved that money alone can't build football culture. Japan and South Korea showed that structure, patience, and community engagement matter more than star power. Southeast Asia demonstrated the power of passion—but also the dangers of neglecting governance.

Together, they illustrate that the future of football won't be written in boardrooms—it will be built in stadiums, streets, and schools.

The Takeaway

Asia has become football's final frontier—a place where dreams, money, and politics collide.

For European investors, it's a market of endless growth. For Asian nations, it's a chance to redefine global football on their own terms.

The continent's next challenge isn't importing superstars—it's exporting stability, authenticity, and identity.

Because in football's global race, the East doesn't need to imitate the West. It only needs to remember what made the game magical in the first place.

As we'll see in the next chapter, the next revolution won't come from geography but from technology. Football's digital transformation—from streaming to NFTs to AI—is reshaping how the world plays, watches, and profits from the beautiful game.

Chapter 11 – The Digital Revolution

The Moment Football Went Online

It began quietly, almost invisibly. In the early 2010s, fans started watching highlights not on TV, but on **YouTube**. A decade later, full matches were being streamed live on **Amazon Prime**, **DAZN**, and **Apple TV**.

Football, once tied to stadiums and television schedules, had gone digital.

Clubs realized that their biggest audience wasn't in the stands—it was on screens. The game that once lived in ninety-minute bursts now existed everywhere, all the time. From short clips to memes, from digital collectibles to AI-driven stats, football had become a **24/7 global content engine**.

The digital revolution didn't just change how people watched the sport—it changed what football *was*.

Streaming: The New Stadium

For most of the 20th century, broadcasting rights defined football's economy. Sky's **1992 Premier League deal**, worth £304 million, transformed English football from a local pastime into a global spectacle. But streaming has taken that revolution even further.

Platforms like **DAZN** and **Amazon Prime Video** broke the monopoly of traditional broadcasters. Fans could now watch from any device, anywhere. Smaller leagues—once ignored by major networks—found global audiences through subscription apps.

In 2023, Apple signed a **$2.5 billion deal** to stream Major League Soccer worldwide, setting a precedent for what's next: football as on-demand entertainment.

The result is a shift from broadcasting to **ownership of attention**. Clubs and leagues aren't just competing for viewers—they're competing for screen time against TikTok, Netflix, and Fortnite.

Social Media: The Second Pitch

If the stadium is where football happens, social media is where it *lives*.

Clubs now run massive digital departments, producing daily content for billions of followers. Manchester United, Real Madrid, and PSG all boast more than 100 million followers each.

Every goal, training clip, and locker-room laugh is packaged and posted in seconds. Clubs aren't just teams anymore—they're **media companies** with brand personas.

Liverpool sells authenticity and emotion. PSG sells style and celebrity. Manchester City sells precision and innovation.

Social media has turned fans into marketers, amplifying every piece of content. A viral goal isn't just a sporting moment—it's free advertising that reaches millions within minutes.

But this constant visibility comes at a price. Players now live under digital surveillance, their every mistake magnified and memed. The same platforms that build heroes can destroy them overnight.

Data Is the New Currency

Behind the hashtags and livestreams lies football's invisible engine: **data**.

From scouting to sponsorships, analytics drive modern football. Clubs use machine learning to analyze player performance, fan demographics, and engagement behavior.

Companies like **StatsBomb**, **Opta**, and **Wyscout** provide terabytes of data to clubs across the world. Cameras track every movement, GPS sensors measure sprint speeds, and AI systems predict fatigue or injury risk.

Even fans are part of the data economy. Every time someone buys a shirt, streams a match, or clicks a post, that interaction becomes monetizable insight.

For investors, this data means predictability—reduced risk and optimized decisions. For traditionalists, it's a warning sign: the human element of football is being quantified to death.

NFTs, Crypto, and the Football Gold Rush

By 2021, a new buzzword was everywhere: **NFTs**. Clubs began launching digital collectibles—virtual trading cards, limited-edition videos, and "fan tokens."

Companies like **Socios.com** promised to "democratize fan engagement," letting supporters vote on jersey designs or slogans using blockchain-based tokens.

At first, it seemed revolutionary. Millions of fans bought in. PSG, Juventus, and Manchester City were among the first to adopt the model.

But as crypto markets crashed, enthusiasm cooled. Many fans felt exploited, realizing the "votes" they bought had little real impact. Critics called it "financialized fandom"—a digital version of the commercialization that had already priced many supporters out of the stadium.

Still, the experiment revealed something crucial: football's hunger for **new revenue streams** knows no bounds. Whether through crypto or AI, the sport's business model is now built on innovation—sometimes reckless, sometimes visionary.

The Rise of the Virtual Fan

As technology advanced, football began to merge with virtual worlds.

During the pandemic, when stadiums fell silent, clubs experimented with digital engagement: cardboard cutouts, Zoom crowds, and virtual reality matchday experiences.

Now, that temporary solution is evolving into a permanent feature. Clubs like **Manchester City** and **Barcelona** are investing in **metaverse projects**, building digital stadiums where fans can attend virtual matches, buy NFTs, and interact through avatars.

For global supporters who can't afford to visit Europe, these experiences promise access. For clubs, they offer another form of monetization.

The future fan may never step foot in Old Trafford—but they'll still buy virtual seats, digital kits, and metaverse memberships.

Artificial Intelligence and the New Edge

AI isn't just changing how clubs interact with fans—it's changing how they *play*.

Modern analytics departments use AI to model match outcomes, analyze opposition tactics, and even simulate in-game decisions. Recruitment departments rely on predictive algorithms to identify future stars.

In 2024, several clubs began testing **AI-driven tactical simulations** that generate ideal lineups based on opponent data. Coaching, once an art form, is becoming a science.

Even commentary and content creation are being automated. Some broadcasters now use AI-generated match summaries and highlights to cut costs.

It's efficient—but also unnerving. Football's chaos, its unpredictability, is what made it beautiful. What happens when that chaos is optimized out of existence?

The New Power Players

As digital platforms take over, new kinds of companies are entering football.

Tech giants—**Apple, Amazon, Google, and Tencent**—now hold more sway over football's future than many traditional broadcasters. Their global ecosystems of apps, ads, and devices allow them to shape how billions consume the game.

For clubs, partnerships with these firms bring exposure and data access. But they also bring dependency. Whoever controls the streaming infrastructure effectively controls the game's visibility—and therefore its economics.

The next big power struggle in football might not be between UEFA and breakaway clubs, but between leagues and Silicon Valley.

The Changing Role of the Fan

In the digital age, fandom has become more fragmented. A teenager in Seoul or Lagos can follow Manchester City more closely than their local team. A fan in New York might support three clubs in three leagues simultaneously.

This global fluidity expands football's reach but weakens local identity. Supporters have become **content consumers**, following narratives rather than neighborhoods.

The chant-filled terraces of the past have been replaced by comment sections, emojis, and algorithmic engagement. The emotion remains—but the context has changed.

Between Innovation and Exploitation

The digital revolution has made football more accessible, more data-driven, and more profitable than ever. But it's also blurred the line between innovation and exploitation.

Clubs use algorithms to predict which fans are most likely to buy merchandise. Social media teams design posts for maximum "add-to-cart" conversions. Even nostalgia is monetized through retro shirt re-releases and "classic highlights" playlists.

Football has become a **product ecosystem**—and fans are the data points that sustain it.

Yet, for all its commercialization, the game still produces real emotion. When a goal goes viral or a historic underdog wins, the digital noise quiets for a second, and football feels human again.

The Takeaway

The digital age has turned football into a hybrid of sport, media, and technology. It's more global, more connected, and more profitable—but also less personal.

For clubs, data is power. For tech giants, football is content. For fans, it's a balancing act between passion and participation.

The question is no longer *if* football is digital—it's *who controls* that digital future.

Because as oil money once reshaped the sport's economy, algorithms and AI now threaten to reshape its soul.

And as we'll explore next, the globalization that once promised equality is revealing a darker side—the growing divide between rich and poor clubs, winners and workers, haves and have-nots in the modern football machine.

Chapter 12 – The Hidden Costs of Globalization

The Price of Progress

On a cold Tuesday night in northern England, a few thousand fans gather at a crumbling lower-league stadium. The floodlights flicker, the stands are half-empty, and the club's owner has warned that without new investors, this could be their final season.

A few hundred miles away, in the luxury suites of the Etihad Stadium, champagne glasses clink as Manchester City celebrates another nine-figure sponsorship deal. The same sport, the same country—yet they might as well be different worlds.

This is the quiet contradiction of modern football: the richer it gets, the more fragile its foundation becomes.

The Billionaire Boom and the Vanishing Middle

Globalization has made football a trillion-dollar industry. Broadcasting, sponsorships, merchandise, and betting revenue have created unprecedented wealth. But that wealth flows upward, not outward.

In Europe's top leagues, a handful of clubs dominate both the trophies and the balance sheets. In the Premier League, the "Big Six"—Manchester City, Manchester United, Liverpool, Arsenal, Chelsea, and Tottenham—earn **more than the other fourteen clubs combined**.

TV rights were supposed to level the playing field. Instead, they became a hierarchy multiplier. The global reach of a few elite brands—fueled by streaming, social media, and international fandom—has concentrated attention and money like never before.

Smaller clubs, once sustained by local communities, now depend on survival grants or speculative investors. The middle tier of football—those traditional community clubs that bridged grassroots and glory—is disappearing.

Transfer Inflation and the Arms Race

Nowhere is the inequality more visible than in the transfer market.

When **Zinedine Zidane** moved to Real Madrid for €75 million in 2001, it was considered astronomical. By 2017, **Neymar's** €222 million transfer to Paris Saint-Germain made that number look quaint.

In the 1990s, a £10 million transfer could change a club's trajectory. Today, it barely buys a promising teenager.

This inflation is driven by the same forces that drive housing markets or tech stocks—competition among billionaires, inflated asset values, and the endless chase for global exposure. Clubs don't just buy players for performance; they buy them for branding, social media traction, and shirt sales.

A footballer isn't just an athlete anymore—they're a **financial instrument**.

The Wage Divide

The top 1% of players now earn more in a week than entire lower-league squads make in a year.

In 2024, **Kylian Mbappé's** reported salary at PSG was over €70 million annually, excluding endorsements. In the same year, players in League Two—the fourth tier of English football—earned a median salary of around £40,000.

The gulf is staggering. At one end, private jets and superyachts; at the other, players juggling part-time jobs or crowdfunding their recovery from injury.

This imbalance mirrors the wider global economy: globalization creates growth, but also disparity. The more football becomes global, the less equal it becomes.

The Exploited Dream

For thousands of young players across **Africa, South America, and Eastern Europe**, football represents a ticket out of poverty. But that dream often comes with exploitation.

Unregulated academies promise trials in Europe in exchange for fees families can't afford. Many of these so-called "agents" vanish after taking payment. Others transport minors illegally, leaving them stranded when deals collapse.

According to **FIFA's own estimates**, thousands of underage players are trafficked each year through unofficial channels. Most never reach professional football. Some end up undocumented, working in menial jobs far from home.

For every superstar, there are countless untold casualties of the global football economy—a system that markets dreams while monetizing desperation.

The Global Academy Machine

Even legitimate academies have evolved into **global recruitment networks**.

Elite clubs like **Chelsea, Manchester City**, and **RB Leipzig** maintain extensive scouting systems that span continents. Young players are signed early, loaned across Europe, and tracked like investment portfolios.

For clubs, it's a numbers game: sign a hundred teenagers, and if one becomes a £50 million player, the strategy pays off.

For the players, it's a gamble—one where the odds are brutally low. Many spend their careers bouncing between loan spells before fading into obscurity. Development has become industrialized, and youth has become an asset class.

Agents and the Price of Access

Agents were once middlemen; now they are **power brokers**.

Super-agents like **Jorge Mendes** and the late **Mino Raiola** turned representation into empire-building. They don't just negotiate contracts—they engineer transfers, influence clubs, and sometimes even own stakes in player rights.

Their commissions often exceed millions per deal, and the incentives are clear: more movement means more money.

For smaller clubs, this dynamic is devastating. When agents hold out for higher fees, transfers collapse. When young players are told to chase wealth over development, careers derail.

Football's transfer ecosystem now resembles Wall Street—fast, speculative, and dominated by intermediaries.

Fans Priced Out

Globalization hasn't just changed who owns football—it's changed who can afford to watch it.

Ticket prices at elite clubs have soared far beyond what local fans can pay. A season ticket at **Arsenal** or **Tottenham** can cost over £1,000, compared to less than £200 at many lower-league clubs.

Television, once the affordable alternative, has fractured into multiple streaming subscriptions. Watching every Premier League game in the UK now costs over £100 per month across different platforms.

The irony is cruel: as football becomes more "accessible" globally, it becomes less accessible locally.

The Death of the Local Club

In the shadow of globalization, small clubs are dying.

Teams like **Bury FC**, founded in 1885, were expelled from the English Football League in 2019 after financial collapse. Others—Macclesfield, Oldham, Southend—have faced administration or expulsion.

These aren't just clubs; they're cultural anchors. For generations, they provided identity, belonging, and Saturday rituals. Their disappearance leaves emotional and economic holes in communities already struggling.

When global football celebrates its billion-dollar deals, these are the invisible costs—forgotten towns where the flood of money never reached.

The Worker Behind the Spectacle

Beyond players and fans, there's another group rarely seen: the workers who keep the football machine running.

Stadium cleaners, security staff, and overseas laborers who build new arenas—often under poor conditions and minimal pay. The **Qatar World Cup 2022** spotlighted these issues, with reports of migrant workers dying during construction.

The line between sport and exploitation grows thinner when profit becomes the only goal.

The Mirage of Equality

Football's global reach has made it seem more inclusive than ever. Players from every continent, fans in every country, coverage in every language. But inclusion on screen doesn't equal fairness behind the scenes.

The sport's wealth gap mirrors the inequalities it pretends to transcend. The Champions League feels more like a private club, where new entrants are tolerated but rarely welcomed.

Globalization made football richer, but it also made it more predictable. The same teams win, the same leagues dominate, the same brands sell shirts worldwide.

A Beautiful Game in Chains

The irony of football's success is that it has trapped itself. The sport can't stop growing, because its business model depends on it. Every year, more sponsorships, more matches, more content, more exposure.

But endless growth has consequences. Players burn out. Fans disconnect. Communities crumble.

Football's globalization isn't evil—but it's **imbalanced**. It reflects the same forces shaping our world: consolidation of wealth, corporate control, and the slow erosion of shared meaning.

The Takeaway

The global expansion of football was supposed to democratize the game. Instead, it created an empire with kings and peasants.

From inflated transfers to trafficked teenagers, from billion-dollar stadiums to bankrupt clubs, every success story hides a cost.

Globalization gave football its reach—but took away its roots.

And as the sport's powerbrokers chase new frontiers—like women's football, digital markets, and sustainability—one question lingers: can growth ever be ethical in a game built on inequality?

That's where we turn next—to the rise of women's football, the next great frontier for investors and brands, and a test of whether football can expand without repeating its old mistakes.

Chapter 13 – Women's Football and Corporate Growth

A Night That Changed Everything

On **July 31, 2022**, more than **87,000 fans** filled Wembley Stadium for the **UEFA Women's Euro final**. England faced Germany in a match that wasn't just about silverware—it was about recognition.

When **Chloe Kelly** poked home the winner in extra time, the roar that followed shook more than the stadium. It echoed across a century of struggle, from a time when women were banned from playing football to a moment when they stood at its summit.

For millions watching around the world, that night felt like the beginning of something irreversible. Women's football was no longer an afterthought—it was a global industry in the making.

But as with every new frontier in football, success comes with a question: who benefits most—the players, or the corporations now rushing to invest?

From Ban to Boom

In 1921, the **Football Association (FA)** banned women from using its pitches, claiming that football was "unsuitable for females." The decision effectively killed a thriving women's scene that had drawn tens of thousands of spectators during World War I.

For fifty years, the ban stifled progress. Women played on parks, fought for resources, and built their own leagues in the shadows. It wasn't until **1971** that the FA finally lifted the restriction, allowing women's teams back into official facilities.

The modern women's game emerged slowly, built by passion, not profit. Volunteers, teachers, and community clubs kept it alive through sheer determination.

Then came television, social media, and a new generation of fans—fans who wanted equality, representation, and authenticity.

Suddenly, women's football wasn't a niche—it was a **movement**.

The Corporate Awakening

For decades, major brands ignored women's football. Sponsorship deals were small, media coverage minimal, and wages painfully low.

Then, something changed. The demographics of fandom shifted. Younger audiences—especially women—wanted inclusivity and social responsibility from the companies they supported.

By the late 2010s, brands began to notice the marketing power of representation. Nike, Adidas, Visa, and Barclays saw women's football as both a moral and commercial opportunity.

When **Barclays** became the title sponsor of the **Women's Super League (WSL)** in 2019, it marked the first multimillion-pound deal of its kind in women's football. The partnership was renewed and expanded in 2022 for a reported **£30 million**, cementing the league's professional status.

Similarly, Nike began giving equal prominence to women's kits and players in its global campaigns. For the first time, stars like **Megan Rapinoe**, **Sam Kerr**, and **Alexia Putellas** appeared not as token figures but as icons.

The message was clear: women's football wasn't just an ethical investment—it was **good business**.

The Global Expansion

From the U.S. to Europe to Asia, women's football began scaling up.

In the **United States**, the **National Women's Soccer League (NWSL)** became a blueprint for sustainable growth. Clubs like **Angel City FC** attracted celebrity investors—**Natalie Portman, Serena Williams, Alexis Ohanian**—and filled stadiums through community-driven marketing. The 2023 NWSL final drew record TV audiences, outpacing several men's fixtures.

In **Europe**, Spain's **Liga F**, France's **Division 1 Féminine**, and England's **WSL** have all turned professional. **Barcelona Femení** became the first women's club to sell out the **Camp Nou**, drawing 91,000 spectators in 2022.

Even traditionally conservative markets are catching up. **Japan's WE League**, launched in 2021, was the first fully professional women's league in Asia. African nations like **Nigeria** and **South Africa** are seeing renewed investment after World Cup exposure.

The globalization of women's football mirrors the men's game—but with a fresh sense of purpose and inclusivity.

The Economics of Equality

Behind the surge of support lies a growing debate: **equal pay**.

In 2022, the **U.S. Women's National Team (USWNT)** won a landmark settlement guaranteeing equal pay with their male counterparts. Norway, Australia, and New Zealand soon followed. England and Spain moved toward similar models, standardizing bonuses and per diems across genders.

Critics argue that equal pay isn't financially sustainable yet—that revenue disparities still justify different wage structures. Supporters counter that investment follows visibility, not the other way around. The more money and attention the women's game receives, the faster it grows.

In truth, both sides have a point. Equality isn't just a financial calculation—it's a statement of values. And increasingly, those values drive modern football's commercial success.

Branding the Revolution

Corporations have framed women's football as the face of progress. Campaigns celebrate empowerment, diversity, and breaking barriers. Stadiums light up in rainbow colors. Hashtags trend.

But behind the marketing lies a familiar pattern: **corporate storytelling** that turns activism into advertising.

When brands talk about "changing the game," they often mean expanding market share. The same companies that underpay female athletes in other sports now wrap themselves in feminist slogans.

There's nothing inherently wrong with profit—but the danger is that women's football becomes a **brand exercise** rather than a sporting project. Players become symbols first, athletes second.

The Club Convergence

For men's clubs, launching women's teams has become both a moral obligation and a strategic move.

Manchester United, long criticized for neglecting the women's game, finally relaunched its women's team in **2018**—after years of fan pressure. Chelsea, Arsenal, and Manchester City have invested heavily, integrating their women's sides into their global marketing operations.

It's smart business. Every women's team adds brand goodwill, sponsorship reach, and PR resilience. It also futureproofs clubs against criticism in an era where gender equality is both a social and economic expectation.

But this integration comes with a risk: dependence. Many women's teams rely on the finances of their men's counterparts. If those priorities shift, funding can vanish overnight.

The Human Side of Growth

Beyond the headlines, the women's game remains fragile. Wages are improving but still modest outside elite clubs. Some players in top

European leagues earn less than the catering staff at their stadiums. Others hold second jobs to afford rent.

The 2023 World Cup in Australia and New Zealand shattered attendance and broadcast records, yet several national teams—like **Jamaica** and **Nigeria**—publicly protested unpaid wages and poor facilities.

This duality defines women's football today: global visibility, local struggle.

The Digital Equalizer

One key difference between the rise of men's and women's football is timing. The women's game has grown **during the digital era**, giving it tools that didn't exist before.

Players build massive followings on **Instagram**, **TikTok**, and **YouTube**, bypassing traditional media gatekeepers. Clubs stream matches directly to fans. Brands collaborate with athletes as influencers, not just employees.

This democratization of exposure means a talented 19-year-old in Sweden or Nigeria can reach global audiences overnight. It's football's version of direct-to-consumer marketing—and it's changing who holds power in the industry.

Avoiding the Same Mistakes

As investment floods in, one question looms: will women's football repeat the men's game's mistakes—commercial excess, inequality, and detachment from fans?

So far, the signs are mixed. The culture around women's football remains more community-focused, family-friendly, and socially conscious. But as TV rights and sponsorships skyrocket, the same market pressures that reshaped men's football are already emerging.

The next decade will test whether women's football can stay true to its roots or whether it will be absorbed into the same machinery that once ignored it.

The Takeaway

Women's football is both a **revolution and a reflection**. It's rewriting history while navigating the same forces—money, media, and power—that define the modern game.

Corporate interest has elevated visibility, improved conditions, and inspired millions. But it also risks turning authenticity into advertising.

The challenge ahead isn't whether women's football can make money—it already does. The real question is whether it can grow **without losing what made it different**: community, humility, and joy.

Because if the women's game can find that balance, it might do more than catch up with men's football—it might save it.

Next, we look at the shifting sands beneath football's greatest financial engine: oil. What happens when the fuel that built modern football begins to run dry—and how will the sport adapt in a post-oil era?

Chapter 14 – What Comes After the Oil Era?

The Empire Built on Oil

When **Sheikh Mansour** bought **Manchester City** in 2008, few realized how much that deal would redefine global football. What began as one club's transformation became the blueprint for an entire industry powered by oil wealth.

The City Football Group, backed by Abu Dhabi's vast resources, turned Manchester City into a superclub—and then replicated the model worldwide. **Paris Saint-Germain**, owned by **Qatar Sports Investments**, followed in 2011. **Newcastle United**, acquired by **Saudi Arabia's Public Investment Fund (PIF)** in 2021, became the latest jewel in the Gulf's sporting empire.

For over 15 years, oil money has shaped the modern game: inflating transfer fees, redefining success, and giving geopolitics a front-row seat in sport. But what happens when the oil stops flowing—or when the world moves on from it?

The Carbon Countdown

The world is changing. Governments are phasing out fossil fuels, investors are demanding sustainability, and climate policies are reshaping global economies.

Oil-rich nations know their future depends on **diversification**—investing profits from petroleum into industries that can survive the post-oil world. Football is part of that plan.

Saudi Arabia's **Vision 2030** and Qatar's **National Vision 2030** both treat sport as soft power—a tool to boost global influence, tourism, and prestige long after oil demand peaks.

That's why billions have flowed into clubs, tournaments, and partnerships. But as the clock ticks toward a greener global economy, these investments face a paradox: football's golden age is tied to a resource the world is trying to leave behind.

From Oil to Influence

Oil money in football has always been about more than money—it's been about **image**.

Hosting the **Qatar World Cup 2022** was a masterclass in global branding. For Qatar, it wasn't simply about football—it was about legitimacy. The tournament showcased a modern, ambitious nation while deflecting criticism of its human rights record.

Saudi Arabia's rapid rise in football follows the same playbook. The country has hosted the **Spanish Super Cup**, **Italian Super Cup**, and even boxing and golf tournaments. The goal isn't just diversification—it's **reputation management**.

This is the essence of **sportswashing**: using sport to soften perceptions, build global networks, and reshape narratives.

Yet as sustainability movements grow louder, so do the contradictions. Can a club funded by oil wealth truly commit to a net-zero future? Can the same nations driving carbon dependency rebrand themselves as champions of global progress?

The Green Dilemma

Football's relationship with oil isn't just financial—it's environmental.

Top clubs travel millions of miles a year. Stadiums consume vast energy. Kit manufacturers produce plastic-heavy merchandise. Sponsorships often come from fossil fuel companies.

In an era where industries are judged by carbon footprints, football is under pressure to **clean up its act**. UEFA, FIFA, and domestic leagues have all launched sustainability initiatives, from solar-powered stadiums to carbon-offset travel programs.

But these efforts barely dent the reality. The sport's biggest financial lifelines—Emirates, Etihad, Aramco, and Qatar Airways—are tied to the very resource the world is trying to move away from.

Football's post-oil transition won't just be economic—it will be moral.

New Power Players

As oil's influence wanes, **technology and private equity** are moving in.

Silicon Valley and Wall Street now see football as an under-monetized asset class. Streaming companies like **Amazon**, **Apple**, and **Google** are the new broadcasters. Data firms, AI startups, and investment funds are acquiring stakes in clubs and leagues.

The next financial superpowers in football won't be oil-rich states—they'll be **tech-rich corporations**.

This shift will bring new efficiencies but also new dependencies. If oil-state ownership tied football to geopolitics, tech-state ownership could tie it to algorithms and profit automation. The face of control changes—but the logic remains the same.

Sustainability as Strategy

Some clubs are already rebranding around sustainability.

Forest Green Rovers, a small English club, became the world's first **carbon-neutral football team**, powered by renewable energy and vegan catering. UEFA has praised their model as the future blueprint for eco-conscious sport.

Big clubs are following suit. **Tottenham Hotspur's stadium** uses rainwater harvesting and low-emission systems. **Liverpool**, **Barcelona**, and **Bayern Munich** have pledged to reduce carbon footprints by 50% before 2030.

This isn't just moral signaling—it's marketing. As fans grow more environmentally aware, sustainability has become part of football's new brand identity.

But while European clubs talk about carbon neutrality, Gulf-owned giants continue to expand air travel, stadium construction, and energy sponsorships. The contradictions are hard to ignore.

The End of Easy Money

If oil prices fall or sustainability regulations tighten, the ripple effect across football could be enormous.

Clubs dependent on state backing—like PSG or Newcastle—could face sudden austerity. Transfer markets could cool. Wages could plateau.

In some ways, this might restore balance. The past decade's hyperinflation in wages and fees was fueled by limitless oil wealth. A post-oil era might force football to rediscover **fiscal realism**.

But that transition will be painful. Once you've built an empire on infinite spending, restraint feels like decline.

Football's Identity Crisis

The end of the oil era forces football to ask a deeper question: what should the sport stand for?

In theory, sustainability and ethics could become the new currency of credibility. In practice, financial survival still trumps ideals. Clubs will continue to chase whoever can pay the most—whether that's a sovereign fund or a tech conglomerate.

The moral debates that began with oil money will only evolve. Tomorrow's controversy won't be about fossil fuels—it'll be about data mining, AI sponsorships, and digital rights.

The question isn't whether football can escape its dependence on oil—it's whether it can escape **its dependence on power**.

The Takeaway

For two decades, oil money reshaped football's landscape—building empires, buying loyalty, and redefining ambition. It gave us modern superclubs and record-breaking spectacles.

But the very resource that fueled football's golden age is finite—economically and ethically. As the world transitions toward green energy, the game must confront its next challenge: how to stay rich without staying dirty.

The post-oil era won't end football's global dominance, but it will test its soul. The clubs that thrive will be those that reinvent themselves—not as political symbols or vanity projects, but as sustainable, transparent, and human-centered institutions.

Because when the oil runs dry, the only currency left will be **trust**.

And in the final chapter, we'll explore what comes next—the future of the world's game, shaped by fans, technology, and a long-overdue reckoning with football's past excesses.

Chapter 15 – The Future of the World's Game

The End of an Era, the Start of a Reckoning

Football has always been a mirror. It reflects who we are—our economies, our politics, our ambitions. In the past century, it's mirrored everything from industrial working-class pride to billionaire excess and state-backed empire-building.

But as the world faces new realities—climate change, digital disruption, shifting demographics—football stands at a crossroads. The sport that once sold passion is now a global industry worth hundreds of billions. The question is no longer *whether* football will change. It's *how*—and *who will control* that change.

The next era of football will be shaped not just by players and managers, but by algorithms, fans, and ethics. The game is being rewritten in real time.

From Stadiums to Screens

The future of football isn't confined to bricks and seats. It's streaming, augmented reality, and **interactive fandom**.

By 2030, most major leagues are expected to move toward direct-to-consumer platforms, bypassing broadcasters entirely. Imagine subscribing not to Sky Sports or DAZN, but directly to "Manchester United TV" or "LaLiga Global," with AI-curated highlights and real-time tactical breakdowns.

Virtual reality will turn living rooms into front-row seats. Fans will be able to "sit" in digital stadiums beside avatars of friends across continents. Clubs like **Manchester City** and **Barcelona** are already investing in **metaverse experiences**, allowing fans to explore virtual museums and training sessions.

The matchday experience is becoming as much about the *interface* as the pitch. Football's next big competition might not be between clubs—it might be between **platforms**.

AI Managers and Algorithmic Tactics

Artificial intelligence is poised to become football's invisible coach.

Clubs already use AI for recruitment, scouting, and injury prediction. The next step is tactical simulation—AI analyzing every movement to recommend live in-game adjustments.

By the mid-2030s, we could see AI-assisted coaching become standard, blending human intuition with data precision. Some analysts even predict AI-generated "shadow matches" that test dozens of tactical variations before kickoff.

For fans, this means unprecedented insight. For purists, it raises an uncomfortable question: can a sport defined by emotion survive total optimization?

The Rise of the Ethical Fan

If the last two decades were about commercialization, the next will be about **accountability**.

Modern fans aren't passive consumers—they're investigators, activists, and shareholders in spirit. The backlash to the **European Super League** proved that fan power still matters. Protests, boycotts, and online campaigns can now derail billion-dollar plans overnight.

Future generations, raised on transparency and sustainability, will demand more from the clubs they love. They'll want clean energy, fair wages, local investment, and community involvement. Clubs that fail to adapt will find that no amount of trophies can repair broken trust.

In short, football's next competition isn't just for titles—it's for **credibility**.

The Return of Fan Ownership

Across Europe, a quiet counter-movement is growing. In Germany, the **50+1 rule** still gives supporters majority control of clubs like Bayern Munich and Borussia Dortmund. In England, fan trusts are reclaiming heritage teams—like AFC Wimbledon and Exeter City—through community ownership models.

Technology may soon make fan ownership scalable. Blockchain and digital cooperatives could allow millions of supporters worldwide to collectively buy stakes in their clubs, vote on governance, and hold boards accountable.

The 21st century could see the rebirth of football's founding ideal: that clubs belong not to corporations or states, but to the people.

Women's Football: The Real Growth Frontier

The women's game will be the **engine of football's next expansion**.

By 2030, analysts project the global women's football economy could exceed **$15 billion** annually. Leagues are becoming more professional, players more marketable, and audiences more diverse.

For brands, women's football represents a fresh, inclusive narrative—sport as empowerment rather than excess. For fans, it's a chance to build a new culture before it's corrupted by the same old flaws.

If managed ethically, the women's game could become football's conscience: global, progressive, and grounded in values the men's game has too often lost.

Football and the Global South

While Europe remains the sport's commercial core, the future of football's soul lies elsewhere.

Africa, Asia, and Latin America continue to produce the world's most gifted players—but often see little of the wealth they generate. That imbalance is slowly shifting. New leagues in **Nigeria, India**, and **Indonesia** are investing in youth development and infrastructure.

With streaming bypassing old gatekeepers, these markets can finally tell their own football stories, build local heroes, and retain talent. The next global superstar might not come through a European academy at all.

In the future, the sport's center of gravity may no longer be London or Madrid—it could be Lagos, Jakarta, or São Paulo.

Football Meets Climate Reality

The climate crisis will force football to confront uncomfortable truths.

By 2050, rising temperatures and air pollution could make outdoor play unsafe in parts of the world. Sea level rise threatens coastal stadiums. Carbon-intensive travel schedules are unsustainable.

FIFA and UEFA are already experimenting with "green scheduling" to reduce travel distances, and future World Cups may prioritize environmental sustainability over spectacle.

Football won't escape the planet's limits—it will have to adapt to them. Clubs that ignore the climate question risk not just criticism, but extinction.

Private Equity and the Next Bubble

As oil fades, private equity is taking its place. Firms like **CVC Capital Partners** and **Silver Lake** already own stakes in major leagues. They promise modernization and efficiency—but their goal is short-term profit, not long-term stability.

Football could soon face another financial reckoning, as speculative investment collides with sporting reality. The danger isn't collapse—it's **consolidation**. A handful of investment giants may end up controlling dozens of clubs and leagues, turning the game into a managed portfolio rather than a living culture.

Unless regulators act, football could become just another financial product.

The Human Element

Despite all the change—AI, streaming, billionaires, and brands—the one thing that keeps football alive is **emotion**.

No algorithm can replicate the electricity of a last-minute goal. No investment fund can quantify the tears of a lifelong supporter. Football remains, at its core, the simplest drama ever written: hope, fear, joy, and despair—played out in ninety minutes.

That human connection is both fragile and priceless. It's what every owner, sponsor, and policymaker risks forgetting when they chase growth at all costs.

The Takeaway

The future of football will not be decided by technology or money—it will be decided by meaning.

If the sport continues down the path of unchecked commercialization, it may lose the magic that made it the world's game. But if it learns from its excesses—if it rebalances power between owners and fans, players and profit—it could become something better: **a global community built on fairness, inclusion, and purpose**.

Football began as a working-class pastime and became a billion-dollar business. Now, it has the chance to evolve again—into a force for unity in a divided world.

Because for all its flaws, football still belongs to the people. And no matter who owns the clubs, who sells the rights, or who builds the stadiums, the truth remains the same:

When the whistle blows and the ball moves, the game belongs to everyone.

Printed in Dunstable, United Kingdom

71998041R00060